HIDDEN
HISTORY
of
NEW ORLEANS

Josh Foreman and Ryan Starrett

FOREWORD BY KATY SIMPSON SMITH

THE
History
PRESS

Published by The History Press
Charleston, SC
www.historypress.com

Front cover: Dokwerker op de kade van New Orleans, by George François Mugnier, circa 1880–1888. *From Rijksmuseum.*

First published 2020

Manufactured in the United States

ISBN 9781467143813

Library of Congress Control Number: 2019951979

This book is dedicated to:

Dr. Rafael Rondon (February 14, 1968–November 16, 2015), a philosopher, teacher and friend, who now regales the saints with an endless array of jokes and stories and fills the halls of heaven with his infectious laughter.

Finn Blaylock (November 14, 2011–August 22, 2019), an adventurer and warrior who united a community during his valiant struggle against cancer and was then welcomed into a better world by a fellow fisherman. He now runs about exploring heaven's trails, forests and rivers.

Sam Freeman (October 12, 1975–June 29, 2018), who marvels from afar at an earth traveling sixty-seven thousand miles per hour around the sun.

CONTENTS

Foreword, by Katy Simpson Smith   7
Preface   9
Acknowledgements   11

1. Memories of Penicaut: A Frenchman Finds Adventure
      in Louisiana   13
2. Sinners and Saints: The Parallel Lives of Michel Degout
      and the Ursuline Nuns   27
3. *Amor Omnia Vincit*: Even an Invincible Redcoat Army   41
4. The Duelists: Clara and the Beast   53
5. Pierced with Slander's Venomed Spear: The Sad Tale
      of Cap Murphy and Recorder Ford   71
6. Liberia or Bust: Robert Charles Versus New Orleans   85
7. From Deepest Tartarus: The Axeman and the Birth of Jazz   99
8. Dynamite Bandits: Terrorist Tactics in the Carmen's Strike
      of 1929   115
9. Mosquitoes and Torpedoes: New Orleans Goes to War   129
10. Lavender Line: Tennessee Williams and Gay New Orleans   145
11. Gumbo: Vignettes from New Orleans's Food History   157

Notes   173
Bibliography   185

FOREWORD

The city of New Orleans has no singular history. Studying its past three hundred years requires a sideways approach—how it sprang from swamp and braided the paths of Indians, blacks and Creoles, how it tossed between European powers and retained its un-American charm, that inexplicable disregard for time. To describe a "hidden" history is to acknowledge that what we see is always planted on something unseen. The bright colors of Mardi Gras mask an old insistence on segregation; the savor of gumbo stems from forced migration. New Orleanians keep climbing on top of tragedies, witnessing and remembering and moving on.

Starrett and Foreman introduce us to André Pénicaut, who stumbled upon the bayous and forests beside Lake Pontchartrain before the French began hacking away at the wilderness, replacing a floodplain with one hundred log cabins. From the first strangeness of houses on top of marsh, the city has defined itself by contrasts, the way "Piety Street runs parallel to Desire Street." The proselytizing generosity of the Ursuline nuns pushes up against the determination of early residents to murder one another. The system of plaçage allows for the concubinage of free women of color but also their rise to the ranks of property owners.

Violence runs through this dichotomous history like groundwater. Union general Benjamin Butler hangs his enemies, while the secessionist women of the city weaponize spit and sneers and overflowing chamber pots. Lynch mobs take over the scales of justice. Jazz barely outlasts the Axeman murders. Striking streetcar workers throw dynamite at trains. Tensions shift between the overclass and the underclass. An LGBTQ community that thrived in a shadow world begins to push into the open. That's the flip side of disorder, though it works unevenly, it sometimes ensures that everyone has a stake in this town—not just the corrupt politicians and patricians on St. Charles but also the women of Storyville and the men who ran bars, the "hoodlums" and the "poltroons."

New Orleans today is creaking under the pressure of another inevitable era of change. After Katrina rearranged the maps, moving silt and foundations and families, the city has become wealthier and whiter and no less dangerous for hospitality workers, buskers, young men of color. The river continues to lap at our walls, and the drains cannot hold the new deluges. This has always been a city of centers and margins, and to survive beyond these crises—of housing, of violence, of climate—we must first honor the margins. Listen to the back-of-town. Let the trumpets play loud and late. Find where the water seeps in and give it space.

Perhaps the eighteenth-century Ursuline Sister Saint Stanislaus best described the morbid joy of being a New Orleanian: "All of these little troubles are trying at the time, but one is well recompensed for it in the end by the pleasure one takes in telling of them." What Starrett and Foreman offer here is that humble historical dance: honoring a city's multitudes rather than threading a single narrative. The hidden history of New Orleans is in fact its most authentic one; here, the underbelly is the raison d'être, and the unspoken is what most deserves to be heard.

—Katy Simpson Smith

PREFACE

This work is a collection of eleven little-known—or forgotten—stories from the history of New Orleans. They are by no means exhaustive or definitive. In fact, many of these chapters are open to alternate interpretations, and every chapter can be expanded and improved. It is our hope that these brief stories spark a more general interest in New Orleans's rich history and lead to more scholarly development.

ACKNOWLEDGEMENTS

We would like to thank all those historians, researchers, archivists, teachers, artists and photographers who came before us and paved the way for a project like this. We thank them for allowing us to stand on their shoulders to see the history of New Orleans through their own work.

We would like to extend a special thanks to those directly involved in our project—Joe Gartrell, acquisitions editor at The History Press; Katy Simpson Smith, one of America's finest writers, who very generously took a break from her score of other projects and wrote the forward and offered valuable editing advice; Hayley Behal, editor at The History Press; the Mississippi Department of Archives and History; the University of New Orleans; Mississippi State University; newspapers.com for creating such an amazing research tool; Richard Starrett for the editing; the Bay Saint Louis-Hancock County Library; the Library of Congress, Metropolitan Museum of Modern Art, Yale University, Rijksmuseum and Internet Archive, for digitizing and sharing valuable documents and artwork from the past; George H. Friedman for the images of the 1929 New Orleans carmen's strike; Grace Walker for help translating the seventeenth-century French; and our families, especially our wives and children, Melissa Hubley, Keeland and Genevieve Foreman and Jackie, Joseph Padraic and Penelope Rose O. Starrett. Thank you.

I

MEMORIES OF PENICAUT

A Frenchman Finds Adventure in Louisiana

C'est un jeune garcon—It's a young boy
S'en allant à la voile—Sailing
La chantant tout au long—Singing all the way

Pour y faire un long voyage—To make a long voyage
Aller aux pays hauts—Go to the high countries
Parmi tous les sauvages—Among the wild ones

Ah! Que l'hiver est long—Ah, winter is long
Que ce temps est ennuyant!—the time is boring
Nuit et jour mon coeur soupire—Night and day, my heart sighs

Quand le printemps est arrivé—When spring arrived
Les vents d'avril soufflent dans nos voiles—April winds blow in our sails
Pour revenir dans mons pays—To return to my country

Adieu, tous les sauvages—Farewell, all wild ones
Adieu, les pays hauts—Farewell, high countries
Adieu, les grand's misères—Farewell, big miseries[1]

—From "La Plainte du Coureur-des-bois"
("The Complaint of the Runner of the Woods"),
a seventeenth-century French Canadian song about life on the frontier

Andre Penicaut climbed from his makeshift bed, the sun still an hour from rising. The young man looked over at his *chaloupe* (the French version of a Viking longboat), which was banked on the shore of the little island he and his companions had named Isle-aux-Pois. *We need to get moving*, he thought. *Before the gnats wake up.* The little bloodsuckers had tormented him and his companions since they'd arrived in Louisiana a few weeks before.

He climbed into the boat with the rest of the crew—eight or so other Frenchmen who'd volunteered for this journey of exploration and a few Biloxi Indians—and the men pushed off into the creek that had carried them to the small island. They rowed through wild country dotted with herons. Their Biloxi guides told them where to go and how to find the river prize they'd been seeking: the *Missicipy*. They traveled for a few miles, and their chaloupe glided into open water. Whenever the wind permitted, they took a break from rowing and let the small sails on the chaloupe propel them.

Traveling west, they were funneled into a narrow channel, the banks on either side made from piles of white shells. Then, again, they hit open water. But this time they were not traveling along the Gulf Coast—they had entered a vast lake, which they estimated was twenty-four miles wide. There was some discussion about what they should name the lake. Penicaut's friend Jean-Baptiste Le Moyne de Bienville decided it should be called Pontchartrain, after a powerful man back home.

The crew traveled along the shore of Lake Pontchartrain until their Biloxi guides directed them to bank their chaloupe and make camp—the Mississippi was near. They slept in the swamp that night. The next morning, the group split up. Some men stayed behind with the chaloupe while others, including Penicaut, went ahead on foot. As he waded through swamp, Penicaut marveled at the towering trees that rose from the still water of the bayou. The cypress groves gave way to stretches of tall marsh grass. The Frenchmen's guides, with fox- and otter-skin quivers bouncing on their backs as they walked, told them that the grass produced a fine grain for soup.

Penicaut trudged through the grass, trusting that his guides were right about the Mississippi. He wasn't afraid to trust, but he kept his gun loaded and ready. Always. Then he saw it—for what seemed like a mile, the river stretched out. On either side of the river, the shore was covered with hardwood trees: oak, ash, elm and others unfamiliar to the Frenchmen. They had done it. They had found a route to the Mississippi River from their base at Biloxi. Penicaut filled a cup with river water and took a drink—how sweet it tasted.[2]

Kanonneersloepen in de Dordtsche Kil, by Reinier Vinkeles, 1793. *From Rijksmuseum.*

Penicaut had not only discovered an access point to the Mississippi River that day, he had also discovered New Orleans, or the land that would become New Orleans some two decades later. The descriptions he published of the place are some of the earliest ever recorded and give a first-person look at the untamed land that New Orleans was built on.

Penicaut and his companions made camp underneath one of the Mississippi's great trees. As they sat there, a flock of turkeys roosted in the boughs above them. They were thirty pounds or more each—bigger than any fowl Penicaut had seen back in France. Penicaut and his friends readied their guns and blazed away. Turkeys began to fall, but the rest of the flock stayed in the trees above them. The birds had never heard gunfire before, so they weren't scared off by the sound.

The feast that followed was a fitting reward for the risk and the rowing. Having located the Mississippi, Penicaut and his companions headed back to Lake Pontchartrain, then on to Biloxi with their boats loaded with game. He was eager to report back to his party that his expedition into the wilderness had borne fruit.[3]

It wouldn't be the last time. Penicaut would continue to journey from Biloxi, and then from other points in French Louisiana, to the frontier, taking careful (if only mental) notes of what he saw and experienced. He stayed in Louisiana long enough to actually witness the founding of New Orleans. Later in life, after he had returned to France, Penicaut published his memoir of his time in Louisiana. The memoir tells not only of his first sighting of Lake Pontchartrain and the Mississippi but also of the strange people he met along the way, of wild animals, feasts and dances, murders and betrayals, women, trysts, travel and adventure.

The memoir tells the story of a young man who had grown "passionately fond of rambling" and wanted nothing more than to find adventure; a frontiersman who could live "off the end of his gun" and was so apt at learning languages that he became a translator between the French and Indians; a middle-aged man who had acquired land and a family and couldn't risk quite as much as he once could; a broken-down man desperate to once again cross the Atlantic and return to the wild land of his youth. Penicaut was one of the earliest chroniclers of Louisiana and New Orleans, and to understand the strange and swampy land from which the Crescent City sprang, it's necessary to first turn to him.

⌐—··—⌐

IT MAKES SENSE THAT when Andre Penicaut, as a boy of fifteen, had a "great urge" to go on a journey, he looked west across the Atlantic Ocean. Penicaut was born in the coastal city of La Rochelle, a French hub of trade in the late 1600s. La Rochelle, located about midway down the Atlantic coast of France, was already doing the bulk of the trading with French Canada when King Louis XIV and his ministers decided to make the city a kind of state-sponsored military and economic powerhouse in 1666. France founded the walled city of Rochefort about twenty miles south of La Rochelle that year. The goal was to make Rochefort a premier French naval base—one that could draw on the population, supplies and financial services of nearby La Rochelle. La Rochelle, in return, was granted a monopoly on trade with Canada. So, Penicaut grew up in La Rochelle at a time when the city was becoming the gateway to France's new-world holdings for both trade and military excursions.[4]

Iberville's 1698 voyage to Louisiana, which first took Penicaut to the New World,[5] had a decidedly martial feel. Upon arriving at Biloxi, the first thing the Frenchmen did was build a fort, though it would soon be replaced with

From an Original Drawing of Piazzettas in the Collection of Joseph Cradock Esqr to whom this Plate is inscribd by his most humble & Obedient Servant J.Bretherton.

Man in a Fur Hat Holding a Musket, Looking Upwards, by James Bretherton. *From Metropolitan Museum of Art.*

a larger and more heavily fortified one, on the Mobile River. The English and Spanish were also eager to establish footholds in the New World, and run-ins with the French were sometimes violent. Iberville's expedition to the Gulf in 1699 had actually passed by a half-finished, months-old Spanish fort at Pensacola. The Spaniards gave the Frenchmen a frosty reception, asking that they stay on their boats in Pensacola Bay (later, full-scale hostilities would erupt between the French and Spanish here).[6] The various Indian tribes that Penicaut encountered would prove to be hostile from time to time as well. Penicaut would write in his memoir that powder and shot were "absolutely necessary" when traveling in Louisiana.[7]

Penicaut had left France in search of adventure, and he found it immediately upon arrival in the New World. His adventure often took the form of boat trips up and down the Mississippi. On his trips, he would go from Indian village to Indian village, talking to, dancing with and occasionally escaping from Indians. Much of the early part of Penicaut's memoir describes the Indians who occupied southern Louisiana at the time of French contact.

He wrote of the Pascagoula, who would strip to cope with the August heat. The Pascagoula men would go completely naked and the women would wear a two-foot-long hank of moss between their legs, which the French jokingly called a "Spanish beard" (the Spanish called it a "French wig" in return).[8] Penicaut wrote of the Houma and Bayagoula, who were fiercely protective of their respective hunting territories and erected a red-painted stick at the border of the two nations, sixty-odd miles from New Orleans. This gave the name to the city that would become Baton Rouge.[9] He wrote of the quarrelsome Alibamons, who acted as a buffer between the French holdings of the Gulf Coast and the English colonies of Carolina.[10]

During his time in Louisiana, Penicaut learned to speak Indian languages. He came to the New World as a carpenter, but he soon grew into a frontiersman and translator. He spent days, weeks and months at a time in Indian villages. In 1700, on his first ascent of the Mississippi, Penicaut and his crew pulled into sight of Cahokia, the former center of one of the greatest Indian civilizations in North America: the Mississippians. Cahokia was just off the Mississippi River in present-day southern Illinois. The Mississippians had abandoned the city by the time Europeans reached the New World, but Indian tribes such as the Illinois still lived in the area. Penicaut and his companions made a grand entrance the first time they reached the site.

"We headed in under sail," Penicaut wrote, "Firing ten or twelve canister shots, at which the savages were greatly surprised."

Once Penicaut made land, he too was surprised. He found thirty French Canadian fur traders and three French missionaries living among the Indians (run-ins with other Europeans on the frontier were neither common

Mural depicting the meeting of the French and the American Indians. *From Library of Congress.*

nor rare). Penicaut and his crew, for whom the journey up the Mississippi had not been easy (they had run so low on food at one point that they were subsisting on tree shoots and sap), stayed with the Illinois for two and a half weeks. When it was time to go, four of the Frenchmen who'd accompanied Penicaut headed north to Canada, and five of the French Canadians headed south with Penicaut.[11]

Penicaut was fond of writing about food and included many descriptions of the game-centric cuisine that the French encountered in Louisiana. The Frenchmen were often "living off the ends of their guns" as they explored. They primarily ate plump turkeys, whitetail deer, buffalo, bear, fish, wading birds and the Indian dish called sagamite (a soup made from grain, vegetables and meat). At Bay St. Louis, between Biloxi and Lake Pontchartrain, the men had hunted the wild and woolly bison, which at the time of European contact roamed from Louisiana to Florida in great numbers.[12] After ascending the Mississippi in 1700, Penicaut and his companions wintered in present-day Minnesota, huddling in huts for months, subsisting on the four hundred bison they had killed for provisions. Penicaut wrote that at first eating such great amounts of bison made him and his companions sick, but after a few weeks of the diet, they were each eating more than ten pounds of meat and drinking four bowls of bison broth a day.[13]

In the village of the Colapissas—one of Penicaut's favorite tribes, whose language he learned to speak—on Lake Pontchartrain, Penicaut and his friend Picard, a fiddler, spent an entire night in 1706 playing music and dancing and woke up late the next morning to a feast of fish "fricasseed" in bear fat, strawberries and sagamite. It was served by the village chief's two comely daughters.[14]

Trips to the Indian villages provided Penicaut with the adventure he so craved as a young man—and brought him closer than he may have liked to becoming a forgotten French explorer killed on the frontier.

Penicaut perhaps came closest to meeting his demise in 1714 on another trip up the Mississippi. He and his party had stopped at the village of the Natchez Indians (where Penicaut would later buy property) on their way up to the Illinois country. They stored some trading goods at a crude warehouse in the Natchez village and left the reluctant Chevalier de la Loire behind to look after the goods.

The grand chief of the Natchez provided Penicaut and his party with an escort of eight men for their journey upriver. The men were supposed to help with rowing, but unbeknownst to Penicaut, the Indians had a darker purpose in mind. The Natchez were plotting to lead the Frenchmen into an ambush upriver where they would be robbed and killed by a small army of 150 Natchez warriors. Penicaut learned of the planned betrayal in a quiet moment from a guilty Natchez escort:

> *While we were camped on the river bank, one of the eight savages came and sat down close to me and, after asking me for a pipe to smoke, which I gave him, he whispered to me in such a way that I alone heard him: "Where do you think you are going, Frenchman?" I replied: "To the Illinois." But, after thinking a moment, I inquired why he had asked me that question. The savage answered that his heart was weeping because we were to be killed the next day.*

Penicaut told his companions, and the Frenchmen turned their boat around and headed south. The seven other Natchez guides admitted to the betrayal and agreed to accept payment in return for staying quiet and letting the Frenchmen head back downriver without hindering them. Penicaut and his men had avoided certain death, but the danger was not over—they still had to extract their friend Chevalier de la Loire from the Natchez village. The Natchez would, presumably, realize that the Frenchmen had become aware of the planned betrayal when they showed up at the village alive and well. Penicaut, speaking to de la Loire's brother, hatched a brash plan to rescue the stranded Frenchman.

"I told him that if he would permit me," Penicaut wrote, "I would go after his brother by myself and would bring him back with me or perish in the attempt."

Penicaut's plan was to walk into the Natchez village alone, pretend that everything was normal, and abscond with de la Loire at night when the Natchez were asleep. The Frenchmen reached the Natchez village in the afternoon. Penicaut climbed out of the chaloupe, his musket slung over his shoulder, and gave instructions to wait until midnight for his return. If he did not return by midnight, the men should presume him dead and leave.

He walked three miles back to the village, thinking about the story he would tell the surprised Natchez to explain why the Frenchmen had come back downstream (and were still alive). When he came in sight of the village, a few Natchez spotted him and alerted the rest of the village's residents. Penicaut told the Natchez that some of his party had grown too sick to travel and had needed to turn back.

De la Loire emerged, and upon seeing Penicaut, ran to him and hugged him. The two men were taken to a hut to sleep for the night with three Natchez warriors. Penicaut quietly explained to de la Loire that the Natchez had been planning to betray the French. "Have your musket loaded and at hand," Penicaut told his friend.

When their three Natchez roommates went to sleep, it was time to take action. Penicaut entertained murderous thoughts ("I was seized with an urge to stab them in the heart with my bayonet.") but decided to slip out of the hut quietly and make for the river. On their way out of the hut, Penicaut barred the door from the outside. They ran all the way back to the river where they met their relieved companions.

Against all odds, Penicaut had rescued his companion and survived. He had been adventuring for fifteen years by that point, and the incident showed him that if not for a little luck and the warning of a guilty traveling companion, he might have died an anonymous death on the banks of the Mississippi. The incident is a high mark of tension in Penicaut's narrative and might represent the point at which Penicaut decided to scale back his adventuring a bit.[15]

In 1718, four years after the Natchez adventure, Penicaut's old companion Bienville was named governor of Louisiana. One of Bienville's goals as governor was to establish a new city on the Mississippi. Journeying with Penicaut up the river two decades before, Bienville had spotted a bend in the river that looked particularly suitable. The crescent-shaped bend had never left Bienville's mind; he called for carpenters to head to the spot (it's unclear whether Penicaut was one of the carpenters who heeded the call) and start building barracks and sheds. Slowly, a sad little settlement began to take shape. Based on Penicaut's descriptions of what was happening in New Orleans, it seems likely that the man was with Bienville in those earliest days.[16]

Another early witness of the birth of New Orleans, Englishman Jonathan Darby, was there when Bienville began clearing cane in 1718. The forty men selected for the clearing of the New Orleans site were a rough lot. Thirty were convicts, six were carpenters and four were Canadians. A couple of officials arrived, and a farmer named Monsieur Dreux established a plantation called Gentilly a few miles away. Penicaut described the supply ship Le Neptune arriving at New Orleans and carrying a "great deal of merchandise and munitions and several soldiers." The boat was helping to fill up the warehouses that were being built. It would also transport a "great number" of families from Dauphin Island—some of New Orleans's earliest residents.[17]

In 1854, another writer, Charles Gayarré, described what New Orleans was like then: "The space now occupied by New Orleans was then entirely covered with one of those primitive forests with which we are so familiar. Owing to the annual inundations of the river, it was swampy and marshy, and cut up with a thousand small ravines, ruts, and pools of stagnant water when the river was low. The site was not inviting to the physical eye, but Bienville looked at it with the mind's vision."[18]

More people moved to New Orleans when war broke out between France and Spain in 1719. Bienville immediately decided to launch an assault on the Spanish fort at Pensacola, only fifty miles from Mobile. The French took Pensacola. The Spanish took it back. And the Spanish decided to attack Dauphin Island, the gateway to Mobile Bay. The Spanish attacked for twelve days, unsuccessfully. The French then counterattacked at Pensacola, again taking the fort. This time they burned it.[19]

The proximity of Mobile to Spanish enemies, who could attack coastal cities from Havana, spurred the French to move farther west and away from the coast toward New Orleans. It was then that the Dauphin Island families moved to New Orleans. Dauphin Island's warehouses were emptied and moved to Biloxi and New Orleans, and all of the troops that had been stationed at Dauphin Island left.[20]

Bayou St. John, a crucial waterway in early New Orleans. *From Library of Congress.*

Penicaut narrated the conflict in his memoir, but whereas in his earlier tales he had taken a central role (as in the escape from the Natchez), in the story of the French and Spanish war, Penicaut seemed detached from the action. He wrote about the large-scale movements of troops and the strategies of each side's military leaders but never mentioned being near any of the action.

The last few chapters of the memoir are almost wholly dedicated to reporting the comings and goings of ships in New Orleans, Ship Island, Biloxi and other French colonial cities. He also described the arrivals of people and where settlers decided to try farming. Some early settlers, such as the king's attorney general Cartier de Baune, settled near Bayou St. John. Three brothers of the Chauvin family moved east from Mobile in 1720, establishing plantations in an area near New Orleans called Choupitoula. The brothers brought one hundred slaves with them, Penicaut noted, establishing a population that would come to define the culture of New Orleans. Other planters followed the Chauvin brothers, settling in the rich farmland between the Mississippi River and Lake Pontchartrain.[21]

Bienville began directing ships from France to unload at New Orleans, where cargo was unloaded and stored in warehouses.

During this time, Penicaut made a map of Louisiana. And it could be this image—of Penicaut leaning over a desk carefully sketching out creek lines, village locations and territorial boundaries—that gives a better idea of what the man was doing in his later years in the colony. Although he scarcely mentioned his family in his memoir, Penicaut did marry while in Louisiana. He also owned property near the Natchez. In the midst of his adventuring, he had accumulated the trappings of settled life.[22]

One of the final notes Penicaut made about the development of New Orleans was that a slave ship called *Le Marechal d'Estrees* had arrived in 1721. The *Le Marechel d'Estrees* was notable for its cargo—175 African slaves who were "allotted to all the residents of New Orleans" upon arrival—but also for another reason. It was the ship that would carry Penicaut back to France.[23]

⌐ ·· ⌐

IN THE FALL OF 1721, Penicaut developed an eye infection and lost his eyesight. He tried in vain to cure his ailment in Louisiana. He made for Paris and again failed to find a cure. He even underwent surgeries, to no avail.[24]

Penicaut had left the Louisiana colony just as the city of New Orleans was sprouting. He would have received updates on the city's progress from other sailors returning from the colony and from letters from friends and family "back home." When he left Louisiana, the site of New Orleans was still covered with "dense canebrake," except for a small space along the Mississippi River where a few log cabins had been haphazardly placed.[25]

He might have learned from travelers that by 1725 New Orleans had grown somewhat, though it was still a backwater. He might have learned that the city now consisted of one hundred crude and haphazardly placed cabins. The town had a storehouse that was sometimes used as a church, a large wooden warehouse and two hundred permanent residents.[26] There were still no levees, and water from the Mississippi flowed into the town yearly. A ditch ran around each square block of the town, and the whole thing resembled a sink that was overgrown with marsh grass.[27]

He might have learned that by 1728 the town had a brickyard. Houses were no longer being constructed from logs but from lumber that was being milled in the land surrounding the town. The combination of brick and lumber changed the appearance of the town. The framed houses were now built on posts with brick chimneys.[28]

But then, maybe Penicaut did not have to hear of New Orleans's progress from seafarers and letters. Perhaps he returned to Louisiana and surveyed the city himself. Penicaut's memoir ends with him sitting in France, a blind man desperate to get back to Louisiana and his wife. But he was still relatively young at the time the memoir was published. If his health improved, he could have easily traveled back to the colonies. And some historians think he did.

The great New Orleans scholar Alcee Fortier believed that Penicaut returned to Louisiana and to his plantation at Natchez. He lived there for several years, the historian argued, again narrowly escaping death at the hands of the treacherous Natchez in 1729. In that year, the Natchez killed more than two hundred French people living nearby in one of colonial America's bloodiest massacres. Penicaut was, according to Fortier, the man who first brought the news of the massacre to New Orleans.[29]

One more adventure for Penicaut and one more close escape. One more contribution to the history of early New Orleans.

SINNERS AND SAINTS

The Parallel Lives of Michel Degout and the Ursuline Nuns

New Orleans is a city of contrasts. It is a city of heroes and villains. Piety Street runs parallel to Desire Street. Jefferson Davis Parkway intersects Martin Luther King Boulevard. The city endorses and promotes mass drunkenness on Mardi Gras, but then the hordes flock to Ash Wednesday Mass the next morning. St. Louis Cathedral is flanked by Pere Antoine Alley (a saintly colonial priest) and Pirate's Alley.

The Crescent City is one of the most violent cities in the United States and is one of the most religious. Its streets are filled with the homeless and destitute, and at the same time, they are filled with some of the fanciest, most beautiful homes in the nation. New Orleans is Treme and the Garden District, simple red beans and rice and elaborate banana foster flambé, Dixie Beer and the Sazerac, Snake and Jakes and Antoine's.

It is, therefore, no wonder that New Orleans's citizens are a mix of sinners and saints. For every Henriette DeLille there is an Axman, for every Ursuline nun, a Michel Degout.

◦———···———◦

IT HAD NOT BEEN an easy passage. What should have taken three months took five. It was a cramped five months too. Thirteen nuns had been forced to share an eighteen-by-seven-foot cabin. Because the odyssey took an additional two months, their food and drink had been rationed. Passenger and nun Marie Madeleine Hachard wrote home to her father, saying, "There were already days in which we were reduced to a pint of water per day. It was the same with wine. The heat was so stifling, and the measure of drink was less than in Rouen. We suffered much from thirst, and that made us exchange our wine for water; however, they only gave us a bottle of water for a bottle of wine. Even then, we were happy to have water at that price."[30]

And then there were the pirates. At least two times, the ship was pursued by pirates. The men aboard the ship loaded the cannons, armed themselves and assumed combat posts. The nuns, meanwhile, huddled in their room and prayed for deliverance. The first time, two corsairs circled the nuns' ship but decided against attacking. The second time, the pirates pursued them for several hours but again called off the chase.[31]

Worse than the pirates were the insects. "Mosquitoes, little animals that I can compare to the ones called bibets or gnats in France, except that their bite is more poisonous and more painful. They cause blisters and painful itching. They take away the skin, and then ulcers come when one scratches. The animals sting with such force that we had our faces and hands covered with their marks, but, happily, these insects appear only after the sun goes down. They reappear the next day at sunset."[32]

After five months of pirates, bugs, dwindling rations and oppressive heat, the pioneer sisters finally arrived in Louisiana. It was an ominous introduction to their new homeland—what would become the death-land of most of the nuns.

The insects, still, were ever present. "Sometimes they come in such great numbers that one could cut them with a knife….They both sting without mercy and their stings are very bad." But the landscape was equally forbidding. "There are only big savage wild woods, inhabited only by wildlife of all colors—serpents, snakes, scorpions, crocodiles, vipers, ticks, and frogs and others that did us no harm, thought they got very close to us. We saw all sorts and in great numbers. The weeds are so high in this place that we could only set our tents on the shore of the river."[33]

When the sisters finally arrived in New Orleans proper, they found a city in its infancy. It was no Rouen or Rochelle, and it was certainly no Paris. Five months before, the nuns had seen the splendors of Versailles. Now, they witnessed the squalor of New Orleans. They didn't even have a convent to retire to. Instead, they would stay at a private residence—the Kolly house—until their convent would be completed seven years later.

Marie Madeleine Hachard, or Sister Saint Stanislaus, took all the sufferings of the early years in stride. She wrote home to her father, "All of these little troubles are trying at the time, but one is well recompensed for it in the end by the pleasure one takes in telling of them."[34]

THE URSULINES HAD BEEN promised a convent before they set sail from France. When they arrived in 1727, there was no convent, though they were promised there soon would be. That promise would be repeated each year for seven years. (They would not move into their promised convent until 1734, when the nuns were able to lead a public procession—in which it seemed all of New Orleans turned out—to their new home.)

In the meantime, while construction was underway (or delayed or ignored), the Ursulines rented the Kolly house, at the intersection of present-day Chartres and Bienville Streets. The owners were absentee landlords who were living in France. However, the husband and son traveled to Louisiana to check on their estates and businesses shortly after the sisters' arrival. Unfortunately for the Kollys, one of their properties was two hundred miles north, in Natchez. Father and son arrived at the concession on November 28, 1729—one day before the Natchez Indians massacred more than two hundred French men, women and children. The Kollys rode toward Fort Rosalie to pay their respects to the commandant. Along the way, they were met by 250 to 300 warriors carrying scalps on their spears. Father and son immediately turned around and fled. The father, Jean, leapt into an empty wine cask. It was suicide. The Natchez saw his desperate attempt to hide, pulled him out and immediately sent him to the netherworld.

Jean's son—and future and hope and beloved of the family—watched his father be assassinated and drew his sword, intent on revenge and survival and a glorious death—or perhaps out of fear and adrenaline and resignation. The Natchez swarmed around him. Seven or eight of them never returned to their village. Nevertheless, the future of the Kollys was captured. Eight days later, he died after a prolongated week of torture by fire.[35]

In the meantime, the Ursulines were fulfilling their duties in the Kollys' New Orleans house. Little did they know that the massacre in Natchez would soon force most of the sisters to reprioritize their daily duties.

The Ursuline Convent in the early twentieth century. *From Library of Congress.*

NEW ORLEANS NEEDED NURSES. The squalid condition of the city and the incessant plagues made a well-run hospital a necessity. The Company of the Indies, therefore, signed a contract with the Ursulines to run the much-needed infirmary. The Ursulines agreed to take charge of the hospital, though the true vocation of their order was not healing but teaching.

The Ursuline nuns came to America determined to teach generations of young French American, black and native girls. They were determined to provide a Christian education to these young women, who, in turn, would pass it on to their own children, thereby Christianizing the continent.

The Ursulines have worked diligently at this mission for three hundred years and counting. Lyle Saxon would later pay the nuns tribute, saying, "The Ursulines played an enormously important part in the early history of New Orleans, for it was in their schools that the future mothers of the colony were educated; it was the Ursulines who took care of the orphans and nursed the sick. Year after year they remained, gaining strength with the growing city."[36]

ON A COLD DECEMBER morning in 1729, a *pirogue* was paddled into New Orleans. It was occupied by half a dozen naked or nearly naked men and women who were splattered with blood. Two were wounded so badly that they had to be helped from the boat. Those who could were screaming or babbling something about Natchez, saying, "Everything was on fire and covered in blood."[37]

Governor Perier immediately summoned the Ursuline nuns. It was time to get to work. New Orleans learned that 144 men, 35 women and 56 children had been massacred in Natchez.[38] The rest of the survivors, and those who would be ransomed, would soon be in the capital.

TWO YEARS BEFORE, THE Ursulines had twenty boarders, three of whom were orphans who were dependent on charity. In addition, a fair number of white children, black people and Indians came for two hours of instruction each day.

The ramifications of the 1729 Natchez massacre for the Ursulines cannot be overstated. Not only were there now scores of orphans (who no one in the city wanted to claim), but also more and more people in the outlying district began to move closer to New Orleans for protection. Everyone feared another massacre.

The city was in a state of collective panic. As often happens, fear led to hatred and a desire for revenge. Worse, it led to the dehumanization of the enemy. New Orleanians reacted violently to the massacre. The brutality of even the women must have stunned the nuns.

THE FIERY PAIN BEGINNING between her legs shot through her body. She had heard the white men talk of hell. Now she understood.

She had been the chief of the Flour Village and had been responsible for the tortuous deaths of a number of the French captives from Natchez. Now the stakes had turned—figuratively and literally, as she was bound to the wooden frame that she was so familiar with.

She had been captured the day before by a band of Tunica Indians, who, in turn, handed her over to the French in New Orleans. She was quickly identified as the chief who had ordered a number of French captives to be either burned or brained. The children were saved for worse torments. They were thrown into the air and then caught by the Natchez warriors on pointed cane spears as their mothers looked on, pleading, shrieking and sobbing. Finally, the children were returned to their mothers, dead. They were placed over an open flame of a spit that their mothers were forced to turn.

When the chief was captured, the French commander immediately ordered her to be executed in the manner of her people. She was handed over to the Tunica to be dispatched…slowly.

She smelled the rank odors of her own burning flesh. Then the smell intensified as smoke began to rise. Still, she looked ahead. There was a smirk of contempt on her face. Occasionally, she shouted out in her native tongue. It sounded like screams to the French, but the Tunica knew better. She was taunting them for their inability to cause her pain. Worse, she was promising revenge when her fellow Natchez learned of her death.

With the chief's nearly entire body now burned, a Tunica warrior stepped forward with a tomahawk and cut a deep, ragged line around her head and then yanked from the top. The upper region of her head came off with ease and was tossed in the sky to the delight of the crowd of French and Tunica in attendance.

Fearing she would expire soon, the French women who had survived captivity among the Natchez were given sharpened pieces of cane. They knew what to do. Some charged the woman who had caused them so much indescribable misery. Others approached calmly, determined to enjoy their moment of revenge. Still others approached with cautious trepidation. Regardless of how the French women approached, the result was the same. The burnt, scalped chief was stabbed repeatedly. She screamed and cursed and flailed. Three minutes later, she was dead.[39]

CRIME, VIOLENCE AND BRUTALITY were commonplace in colonial New Orleans. Torture and death were part and parcel of the world the Ursulines occupied. They could only do their best to curb man's baser instincts. They would do so through the girls to whom they gave a solid, Christian education. They hoped the girls they taught would become pious women who would exert positive influences over their future husbands.

And when those same men committed unto others—and had committed unto them—atrocious crimes, the Ursulines would be there to nurse those who survived said crimes back to health.

And to pray for the souls of the manifold dead.

The Sweetheart statue. *From Josh Foreman.*

THE TRIAL OF MICHEL DEGOUT

February 1, 1766

Michel Degout sat in prison, hands and feet in chains. Things did not look good for the forty-seven-year-old master sculptor. He had been accused of murder one month before in Natchitoches. That was no big deal. That miscreant had gotten what was coming to him. However, there was another case, twenty-two years ago, back in France, that now threatened to destroy him.

———

MARIE DARBANNE DID NOT want to be here, in New Orleans, far away from her husband and home in Natchitoches. But she had been summoned. Or rather, she had been sent.

It was all the fault of Michel Degout. The sooner he was executed, the sooner she could go home. She had already testified against him a month before in Natchitoches. She repeated the same testimony in New Orleans and then reverified her account.

———

THIS WAS NOT AN easy case. Murder or self-defense? He was certainly leaning toward the former, but a man's life was at stake, and he did have a credible story. The question was, what kind of man was Michel Degout? Interrogator Denis Nicolas Foucault was determined to find out.

October 9, 1765

He had been told there would be wine. He liked wine. He really liked wine. But any type of alcohol would do. Especially now.

Why did that damn fool Cratte promise wine and not have it? Well, he would go and get it himself.

He failed. Lemur, a *voyageur* in possession of wine, refused to give him any without a note.

Michel Degout returned to the party empty-handed. Frustrated, Cratte went to get the wine himself. He returned and told Degout to fetch another bottle. Soon after, Degout was on his way back to Lemur's, note in hand. But again, Lemur refused to serve him. Degout returned once more without the wine and, immediately upon entering Cratte's house, began to quarrel with Lemur's friend and fellow voyageur Lemoine. Degout drew one of his sculptor tools with the intention of attacking Lemoine, when Cratte grabbed the sculptor and threw him onto a chest, screaming, "Wretch, you use a weapon?" Lemoine used the opportunity to flee.

But Degout was too worked up to let things settle. He began to pursue Lemoine, with Cratte not far behind.

⌐—··——⌐

SHE WAS FOLDING CLOTHES with her slave Jeanne when she heard footsteps sprinting toward her house. The man leapt onto the porch, stepped over a bed and rushed into the house. It was Michel Degout.

Her husband, Pierre, had allowed the troublesome sculptor to sleep on the porch for a few days, but only a few days. Now Degout was rummaging through one of his chests inside her home. Marie Darbanne asked him what he sought so fervently. No reply. She asked again. Again, no reply. She lowered the laundry and glared at Degout, awaiting an answer. But he kept rummaging through the trunk.

Suddenly, someone else stepped up onto the porch and approached the window.

Degout exclaimed, "Who is there? Is it you, Pierre Darbanne?"

No answer.

"Is it you Pierre?"

"It is I, Cratte."

"Well, here's for you."

Degout thrust something through the window. Cratte screamed, turned and fled.

Marie passed out. When she regained consciousness, she learned that Cratte was dead.

Leogane, France, 1744

Life was grand, especially with a head swimming in alcohol. He was young and strong, with his life before him. And he was drunk.

35

Days later, he was young, strong and marked, with a very different life before him.

Michel Degout had been convicted of stealing three silver pieces. He was whipped through town, branded with a fleur-de-lys and banished. Twenty-two years later, his fleur-de-lys brand would put his life in jeopardy.

February 1, 1766

The man was a branded scoundrel. The little doubt that remained in Foucalt's mind dissipated. Michel Degout was guilty of murder. And he would die a murderer's death.

Foucault and six of his fellow judges drew up and signed the death document. Degout was to be brought to the Place d'Armes with a rope about his neck and a sign attached to his front and back, reading, "Murderer and Assassin." In front of the church, he was to confess his guilt and beg mercy of God and king. He would then be led to the center of the square "to have his arms, legs, thighs and back broken on a scaffold which, for this purpose, shall be erected on the said square, and he shall afterwards be placed on a wheel, to expire there with his face turned toward Heaven until death ensues, his body to be then borne to and exposed on the public road."

MICHEL DEGOUT RECEIVED WORD of his punishment while he was still shackled in prison. He half expected the judgment, but he had still hoped for an acquittal. Now he would be tortured before being fried by the sun.

Fortunately for Degout, there was an addendum to the execution order: He was mercifully to be "strangled under the scaffold before receiving a blow."

The order was carried out verbatim on the same day, February 1, 1766.[40]

MICHEL DEGOUT CAME TO Louisiana with baggage. He wasn't the only one to do so. In fact, colonial Louisiana was populated with the dregs of France. Louisiana needed colonists. Unfortunately, few volunteered to leave France for the unknown and dangerous New World. So, a military police force was hired to empty the streets of vagrants, miscreants and unemployed people. For each undesirable they put on a boat to Louisiana, the captors received one hundred *livres*.

Phase two of the plan to populate the New World required women. Not only were they necessary for future generations, but they would also function as positive and stabilizing influences on the disreputable men. Pierre Le Moyne d'Iberville sent a request to France for women "reared in piety, and drawn from sources above suspicion, who knew how to work."[41] What he got was somewhat different. The French authorities immediately began recruiting and impressing women from the Hôpital Général—a prison for prostitutes. Statistics from the Company of the Indies show that of the 1,215 women sent to Louisiana between 1717 and 1721, more than half were prostitutes.[42]

Finally, when these women (who most believed to be of questionable character) arrived in Louisiana, they were promptly married off to men of equally (perhaps more so) questionable character.

Historian Kenneth M. Myers claims that "in Paris alone more than 4,000 vagrants, prostitutes, smugglers, orphans and other criminals were collected from the streets, jail cells, mental hospitals and orphanages, loaded onto boats, and sent to Louisiana in an ill-conceived ploy to bring civilization to the swampy frontier."[43] In one case, eighty French criminals who had been sentenced to death were given suspended sentences, provided they agreed to sail to Louisiana. Likewise, eighty prostitutes were conditionally released from prison. The convicts were then paired up, shackled together, married in a mass ceremony and sent on their way.

Not surprisingly, many of these marriages failed upon arrival in Louisiana. (Predictably, venereal disease spread rapidly throughout New Orleans and its vicinity.) And their offspring would begin to populate the region. The Ursulines would have plenty of material to work with.

Father Pierre Charlevoix wrote that the early settlers "are wretches, who being banished from France for their crimes or ill-behavior, true or supposed, or who, in order to shun the pursuits of their creditors, listed themselves among the troops, or hired themselves to the plantations…looking upon this country as a place of banishment only, were consequently shocked with everything: they have no tie to bind them, nor any concern for the progress of a colony of which they are involuntary members."[44]

With such settlers populating colonial Louisiana, it should come as little surprise that crime was rampant. Nor is it surprising that early punishments tended toward the Draconian. The execution of Michel Degout was not atypical. In fact, Degout got off relatively easy when he was first strangled.

The altar at the National Shrine of Our Lady of Prompt Succour. *From Josh Foreman.*

The French had experience with the art of torture and execution in the Old World. They brought it with them to the new. Ned Sublette explains some of the various methods employed to keep an unruly people in check:

> *Tearing out entrails from a living victim, pulling apart limb from limb by horses, removing chunks of flesh with red-hot pincers, pouring molten lead into open wounds, flaying alive, bloating alive, slow roasting over a fire, water torture, and the ever-popular ritual of burning at the stake. Across Europe, the hanged—not hung by a quick drop-trap either—but a slow, dangling strangulation—were left on gibbets for crows to pick, set high on the hilltops where they could be seen from all around the surrounding countryside.*[45]

At least some of these tortures were used in colonial Louisiana—on natives, slaves and men like Michel Degout.

THE URSULINE NUNS HAD no authority to stop such barbaric punishments. They could only hope and pray and work to ensure that there would be no need for such punishments in the future. They continued to teach generation after generation of young women of every race and socioeconomic status, in hopes that the young women would one day turn New Orleans into a truly Christian community.

Their mission continues today.

3

AMOR OMNIA VINCIT

Even an Invincible Redcoat Army

The corsair walked along the edge of the Vieux Carre, down Dauphine Street. He slipped by Bienville, Pont, St. Louis, Toulouse, Philip, Orleans and St. Ann. Finally, he snaked his way to Dumaine Street and toward the house he silently sought.

He walked into the front door as if he owned the place. He didn't, but he did pay for it. An attractive, thirty-year-old woman sat dozing in a chair. He lifted her up and eagerly sought her mouth. It had been a while. As soon as she recovered from her sleepy shock, she eagerly returned his kisses.

In the next five minutes, they performed an awkward, passionate minuet with practiced, bumbling hands. The scarf, needed to protect her neck from dirt and dust and soot, was the first to go, then the long gloves protecting her exposed arms were ripped down. Finally, with the shift lying castaway in the corner, the dance became more rhythmic.[46]

⌐—···—⌐

JEAN LAFITTE SAT AMID his plunder and worried about his brother. He had grown close to his brother over the years. Smuggling and piracy and the threat of the noose drew them closer than most siblings. They had sailed together, lived together, created an empire together. And then one day, the affection between them nearly ended. Pierre had suffered a serious heart attack. His health and the warrant hanging over his head worried the younger Jean greatly.

Jean Lafitte—The Pirate from 1883's *Conquering the Wilderness, or, New pictorial History of the Life and Times of the Pioneer Heroes and Heroines of America. From Internet Archive.*

With his brother recovering, Jean had taken over the majority of the Lafitte operations. He was under a great amount of stress, for he had a life-altering decision to make. With his brother making another clandestine visit to New Orleans to visit his mistress, the British navy as powerful force in the Gulf and the American forces as a constant thorn in his side, Jean decided New Orleans had become too hot; he had too many enemies looking to put a noose around his pirate neck. Jean was looking to move his base of operations elsewhere.

And then he got word that a small boat had been detached from a warship and was sailing under a flag of truce straight into the recesses of Jean's stronghold.

⌐—··—⌐

AT LEAST SHE HAD a man who supported her. He paid for her house. He brought her pretty presents from his captured loot. And he had given her a family. A large family. She seemed to be in a perpetual state of pregnancy.

Despite the thrombosis—not to mention the price on his head—Pierre continued to visit her whenever he could. He generally arrived late and left early. And now she was late. Again. It would be their fifth child together.

All in all, it was not a bad life. She had a roof over her head. In fact, several roofs, as her lover tended to stay on the move, mostly to keep away from creditors. She had a couple of slaves. And she had her children. This was about as good of a life a woman with a black mother could have in early nineteenth century America.[47]

⌐—··—⌐

ANDREW JACKSON WAS EXACTLY where he wanted to be—at the head of an American army fighting against the Redcoats. He had hated the British since his youth, ever since he had been slashed across the face with a sword for refusing to polish an English soldier's boots. Now he had his chance.

The only drawback was that he was the general of *this* army. He could trust some of the men, like those who avenged the Creek massacre at Fort Mims with him. Or those who helped take Fort Barrancas from the Spanish and British. Or those who stuck by him on the embarrassing and tedious hikes up and down the Natchez Trace.

But the others? What general could hope to be successful with such a diverse rabble?

Jackson went straight to his headquarters at 106 Royal Street and got to work. The situation looked bleak. New Orleans was a divided city used to shifting allegiances and welcoming various conquerors. Now, an American took defense of the city. Only a few years before, the French and Spanish had alternated rule. Tomorrow, it could very possibly be a British general who was welcomed and feted in the gumbo cauldron that was New Orleans.

Jackson knew he needed to bring the disparate groups together if he was to drive off Napoleon's conquerors. He began by appointing Edward Livingston, husband of Louise Davezac, a former widow from Santo Domingo, as an aide-de-camp. Livingston's connections to the Crescent City's high society proved invaluable. He added a local engineer and architect, Arsene Lacarriere Latour, and local businessman Jean Baptiste Plauche to his rolls, thus ensuring local French support.

Next, Jackson gratefully accepted a battalion of 210 free blacks under the command of a local baker, Jean Daquin. The general insisted that these black men be armed properly and paid the same as their white counterparts. Governor Claiborne and others complained, but Jackson refused to budge. He and New Orleans needed these black men.[48]

Jackson's trusted friend John Coffee brought almost two thousand of the famed Tennessee Volunteers, or as the British labeled them, "the dirty-shirts," with him to New Orleans. The Volunteers, along with nearly eight hundred regular U.S. Army troops would form the backbone of Jackson's army.

Allen and Ginter Cigarettes 1888. *Metropolitan Museum of Art.*

Finally, Jackson mustered in 107 Mississippi dragoons under Major Thomas Hinds, along with 62 Choctaw Indians. As of the first of December, he was still awaiting the arrival of 2,400 Kentuckians under Major General John Thomas and 2,200 more Tennessee Volunteers under General William Carroll.[49]

Jackson's three-thousand-man mixed force prepared to face an army of anywhere from ten to twenty thousand of Wellington's best. Jackson knew it would not be enough. He knew who he needed, and that knowledge filled him with repugnance.

⌐ ⋯ ¬

JEAN LAFITTE CONFIDENTLY STRODE through the French Quarter. He turned onto Royal Street and made his way resolutely to the 100 block, where he found the headquarters of General Jackson. His appearance in the city was a calculated gamble. Many in New Orleans wanted his head for his brazen acts of piracy. But he knew he had something General Jackson desperately needed: Jean himself, his fellow pirates and, just as importantly, weapons. At least that is what he would offer Jackson. In reality, his Baratarian base had just been raided,[50] his operation dashed to shambles, his weapons confiscated, many of his fellow pirates imprisoned, and a warrant put out for his brother, Pierre. Lafitte's Baratarian base, hidden in the swamps south of New Orleans, was no more. It had been attacked and ransacked on September 16, 1814, by the U.S. government. Jean and Pierre, already a wanted man, had leapt into a pirogue and paddled into the swamps to make their escape. Dominique You, like so many other of the Baratarians, was not so fortunate and was taken captive as he tried to flee. But Jean was a calculating gambler, and he was about to pull his greatest bluff. Little did he know that Jackson's position was just as desperate. Jean was badly needed.

Jean had no weapons to offer. In fact, he had almost no men. Most were in prison or running from the law with warrants on their heads. Fortunately, two factors worked in Jean's favor. He had 7,500 gun flints that Jackson sorely needed. In fact, just six days before, Jackson had written to the secretary of war, complaining about the lack of flints. (One particular flint could last anywhere from one shot to weeks of service. Hence, there was a need for multiple flints per soldier.)[51] Lafitte offered to alleviate this concern. Secondly, Jean still commanded the respect of the Baratarians, who were in prison or on the run. He promised Jackson their loyalty (and the flints) in exchange for a general amnesty.[52]

On December 17, 1814, Governor Claiborne issued a proclamation that he and Jackson would do all they could to have the charges against the pirates dropped if they performed satisfactorily in Jackson's army.

JACKSON HAD MADE A deal with the devil. Amnesty for flints. So, when a letter arrived signed by four Ursuline nuns, the general must have been pleased to receive whatever divine help he could. Perhaps the prayers of these religious would counteract his deal with the Lafittes.

Not only did the Ursulines offer their prayers, they had already sent their students out of the city and had ample room to take in and treat those who would be wounded in the coming days.[53]

MARIE VILLARD WAS A product of the colonial French custom of *plaçage*. She was the *placee* of Pierre Lafitte. It was customary for French (and Spanish) men of money to familiarize themselves in the ways of love with a mixed beauty. She could be a mulatto—half white and half "exotic," either black or Indian. She might also be a quadroon—three quarters white. The placee would give her body and affection—sometimes real, sometimes feigned—and in exchange would be set up in a nice cottage. She and her children would be supported by the father. When the arrangement came to an end, as it often did when the white man took a white wife, the property and furniture stayed with the woman, and she could pass it down to her children.

During the decade of Pierre and Marie's tumultuous affair, a young man named Thomas Ashe traveled to New Orleans. He was amazed at the ritualistic and complicated sexual relationships between whites and persons of color. He wrote of nonwhite mothers, "The mothers always regulate the terms and make the bargain. The terms allowed the parents are generally fifty dollars a month; during which time the lover has the exclusive right to the house, where fruit, coffee, and refreshments may at anytime be had, or where he may entirely live with the utmost safety and tranquility. Many do live in this manner, notwithstanding which, I have never heard a complaint against these interesting females."[54]

The practice of sanctioned interracial relationships would continue for several decades after the demise of the Lafitte empire. Harriet Martineau,

Young Woman with a Fan (1906), by Simon Maris. *From Rijksmuseum.*

a British traveler and observer, visited New Orleans in the decade after the end of Pierre and Marie's affair. She described the peculiar practice thusly:

The Quadroon girls of New Orleans are brought up by their mothers to be what they have been; the mistresses of white gentlemen....The girls are highly educated, externally, and are, probably, as beautiful and accomplished a set of women as can be found. Every young man early selects one, and establishes her in one of those pretty and peculiar houses, whole rows of which may be seen in the Remparts. The connexion [sic] now and then lasts for life: usually for several years. In the latter case, when the time comes for the gentleman to take a white wife, the dreadful news reaches his Quadroon partner, either by a letter entitling her to call the house and furniture her own, or by the newspaper which announces his marriage. The Quadroon ladies are rarely or never known to form a second connexion. Many commit suicide: more die broken-hearted. Some men continue the connexion after marriage. Every Quadroon woman believes that her partner will prove an exception to the rule of desertion. Every white lady believes that her husband has been an exception to the rule of seduction.[55]

As misogynistic, racist and class biased as the system was, plaçage did create a platform for a group of people who never before had a sanctioned voice in American society: women of color.

Proof of their newfound agency can be found in the number of those who filed damage claims regarding their personal property after the devastating fire of 1788. Twenty-six free men of color claimed property damage. So did fifty-one free women of color. With all its concomitant negativities, the plaçage system did produce a class of nonwhite women who had, arguably, more agency than any other group of minority women in the country.

More often than not, New Orleans families of plaçage became more and more "white." Soon, a complicated system of legal "whiteness" emerged. Eighty years after Pierre and Marie's trysts, the status of the racially intermingled in New Orleans received a blow with the U.S. Supreme Court's decision in *Plessy v. Ferguson*. In 1897, "separate but equal" became the law of the land. Separate and unequal became the reality. Consequently, there was a great financial and social incentive for persons of color to "pass" as white. (Governor Huey Long would shortly thereafter claim that "pure white people in New Orleans could be fed on a half a cup of beans and a half cup of rice, and there'd be some left over.")[56]

Before his Baratarian base was destroyed by the Americans, Jean was approached by the British. They offered Jean the rank of captain in the British army, generous grants of land once the war was won and amnesty for previous attacks on British ships.[57] Jean asked for a fortnight to consider. He promptly sent a letter to Jean Blanque of New Orleans, a state legislator, merchant, former slave trader and investor in Lafitte privateers.[58] He informed the American of the British offer and expressed his desire to serve his adopted home, the United States. However, he had concerns about casting his lot with the nation that threatened his brother with the hangman's noose. Jean wrote:

> *Our enemies have endeavored to work on me by a motive which few men would have resisted. They have presented to me a brother in irons, a brother who is to me very dear! Whose deliverer I might become, and I declined the proposal. Well persuaded of this* [sic] *innocence, I am free from apprehension as to the issue of a trial; but he is sick and not in a place where he can receive the assistance his state requires. I recommend him to you, in the name of humanity.*[59]

Jean had reason to fear for his brother's life. Pierre had suffered a severe stroke in the fall or winter of 1810. He was only forty years old but was partially paralyzed on his left side and would suffer from periodic and chronic fits of trembling. The historian William C. Davis notes that Pierre's bold and decorative signature forever changed in the spring of 1811—his once bold signature became frail, diminutive and meek.[60] Pierre was forced to limit his travel and extracurricular activities while Jean took over the brother's interests abroad.[61]

Despite his infirmities, Pierre continued his amorous relationship with Marie Villard. Around the time of his stroke, Marie presented Pierre with another child, Jean Baptiste Laffite.[62] One year later, Pierre and Marie added another child, Rosa, to their brood on August 28, 1812.[63] It would be Pierre's devotion to Marie that would nearly doom the brothers Lafitte.

The entire city of New Orleans knew the brothers were smugglers and slave traders. Few cared but some did. Zealous agents were determined to arrest the brothers for violating old revenue laws. Several plots were hatched to apprehend Jean and Pierre.

On the night of July 8, 1814, Pierre was paying one of his conjugal visits to Marie at the house he bought her in her name on Dumaine Street. The authorities made their move, and the partly impaired, yet still vital Pierre was arrested. Unable to make bond, he was placed in shackles in the city jail behind the *Cabildo*.[64] He was placed on the ground floor of a windowless three-story building. His narrow cell was locked from the outside by a swing bolt.

The anti-pirate, anti-Lafitte plotters had gathered dangerous evidence that they planned to present to a grand jury. A number of witnesses had come forward willing to testify as to what they had personally seen on the Lafitte's base at Grand Isle. The prosecution would have an easy time convicting Pierre of piracy. And the fate of a pirate was the hangman's noose. Pierre's days seemed numbered.[65]

The Lafittes' lawyer tried to get Pierre released on account of his health. However, two doctors examined him, and while they admitted that his stroke occasionally caused fits and shaking on his left side, his only issue now was depression. They recommended guarded exercise but that the shackles remain on his feet. The court denied bail.[66]

The same night that Jean sent the British offer to his friend Jean Blanque, Pierre's cell was opened from the outside, and the pirate walked away a free man. As he left, Pierre freed three slaves, and he and his rescuer(s) made their way to Jean at Barataria.[67] No one knew who set Pierre free, but many believed it was Jean Blanque and other merchants who were "involved in the pirate acts he committed and therefore many are interested in saving him at all costs, in order to avoid being discovered."[68] Pierre was free but had a heavy price on his head.

Now Jean was offering Jackson 7,500 flints and the services of the imprisoned and hiding Baratarians in exchange for amnesty for Pierre.

GENERAL JACKSON HESITANTLY ACCEPTED the enlistment of the "hellish banditti" known as the Baratarians. It was a wise decision. Jackson's engineer, Arsene Lacarriere Latour, would later document the Battle of New Orleans in painstaking detail. He paid a number of compliments to the efficacy and importance of the pirates, writing,

> *Mr. Lafitte solicited for himself and for all the Baratarians, the honor of serving under our banners, that they might have an opportunity of proving*

that if they had infringed the revenue laws, yet none were more ready than they to defend the country and combat its enemies.

Some days after, a certain number of them formed a corps under the command of captains Dominique and Beluche, and were employed during the whole campaign at the lines, where, with distinguished skill, they served two twenty-four pounders, batteries Nos. 3 and 4.[69]

Dominique You and his fellow Baratarians did, in fact, affect the outcome of the battle disproportionate to their numbers. The Battle of New Orleans was an affair in which artillery played the dominant role, and the pirates, having at least some experience with cannons, proved to be extremely valuable.

Jean Lafitte led a unit of fifty soldiers to guard the various water approaches to the city. Consequently, he was not present during the actual fighting, but his services as a scout who knew the area better than anyone ensured Jackson that should the British approach from another direction, he would have plenty of time to make adjustments.

The Battle of New Orleans, by E. Percy Moran. *From Library of Congress.*

As for Pierre, he served as an on-site consultant to Jackson because he knew the area's bayous and irrigation ditches. Perhaps his greatest contribution to the battle was to convince Jackson to extend his left flank several hundred yards into the swamp. It proved to be sound advice because at one point the British did try to turn Jackson's flank. The combination of American sharpshooters and thigh-deep swampland forced the British to use their forces in a frontal assault on the middle of the American lines, to disastrous effect.[70]

Had the British not been driven back by Baratarian cannon and flints or stopped by the extended left flank they tried unsuccessfully to turn, the result of the battle and campaign—and indeed the war itself—likely would have been radically different. With control of New Orleans came control of the Mississippi River. The Treaty of Ghent was not yet officially ratified. Thus, the war might have dragged on, with the theater shifting west where Britain could now unite its Canadian and Louisiana forces. Even if the British had captured and returned New Orleans after news of the Treaty of Ghent arrived (and it certainly is a big *if*), the city and its surrounding plantations certainly would have been looted and burned. Britain's own Caribbean islands would have eliminated a chief rival for the next decade.

MARIE VILLARD HAD A role in the drama of 1814 New Orleans. She might have stood in the balconies with those women Latour described: "The fair sex of New Orleans were animated with the ardor of their defenders, and with cheerful serenity at the sound of the drum, presented themselves at the windows and balconies to applaud the troops going through their evolutions, and to encourage their husbands, sons, fathers, brothers, to protect them from the insults of our ferocious enemies."[71] She might have worried over the fate of her provider and lover. She might have prayed daily for his safe return to her and their children. (Then again, maybe she hoped Pierre would not return. Maybe she looked forward to enjoying the property he bought her without the burden of being a concubine.)

Or perhaps she was one of those many women who flocked to the Ursulines' Chapel of Our Lady of Consolation on the night of January 7, 1815, and held vigil before the statue of Our Lady of Prompt Succor. Perhaps Marie was one of those women who filled the chapel to "implore the God of battles to nerve the arm of their protectors, and turn the tide of combat against the invaders of their country."[72]

Regardless of where she was in the days leading up to the climactic battle, Marie played a vital role in the history of her adopted homeland. It was love of Marie, the placee, that drove Pierre to risk his life over and over to visit her at their house on Dumaine Street. It was this need to be in her presence that got Pierre arrested. And it was love of his brother that made Jean rethink the generous British offer and instead offer his services, and those of the Baratarians, to the American cause.

One is left to wonder what would have happened if Pierre had not gotten himself imprisoned, or if he had not fallen in love with his place.

4

THE DUELISTS

Clara and the Beast

Clara Solomon had one, predominant shortcoming: her handwriting. Maybe she had two…or three, if you included her sickliness and her looks.

Her sister, Alice, on the other hand, had no such shortcomings. Her penmanship was exquisite, her looks were breathtaking and she held a good, salaried job as a teacher. Rarely did Alice miss work due to illness. Yes, Alice was the "feminine ideal"—that is, until you looked at "Beauty" Phillips. By the grace of El Shaddai, that woman was a veritable Rachel. She was everything Clara wanted to be. Clara would gladly trade places with either of them.

⸻

HE STARED ACROSS THE harbor at the city he would soon occupy. His stare was really a squint. An involuntary squint caused by two perpetually drooping eyelids. With his strabismus, chubby face and receding hairline, General Benjamin Butler had the look of a tired pug just before its eyes clamped shut. But he was a conqueror. The conqueror of the largest port in the Rebel states and the second largest in America. No, he was not conqueror but liberator. Just like Andrew Jackson. Butler saw himself as the second hero of New Orleans, the preserver of the Union. The conquered would soon give him a plethora of other nicknames.

The Southern Belle, 1872. From Library of Congress.

Maggie wouldn't stop biting her nails. Didn't she understand that she was fighting a battle that would determine her fate? How would she ever land a desirable beau when she abused such delicate hands? Life is full of skirmishes and battles, most minor, but a few can turn the course of the war. Maggie must be encouraged as she battled the temptation to destroy her hands. Fortunately, she had the ideal consultant—Clara Solomon.

Clara noted,

> *I had inspired her with a sense of right in the cultivation of her nails and she was much honored to see the progress they had made, as she had not bitten them for three days. I tried to encourage her in the accomplishment of the noble work, for I know by experience that it is one of the greatest victories which a person can achieve, and I often wonder at myself ever having attained it, but I can attribute it to nothing else than a feeling of pride which maturer age served to develop.*[73]

The general knew how to make money. It was, in fact, his chief talent and primary passion. He had married into wealth. He ran a successful textile empire in Massachusetts. He used his law degree to protect and multiply that money. Now he was in one of the richest cities in the country, with dictatorial powers and almost no oversight. Benjamin Butler stood in high cotton—a commodity that just happened to be desperately needed at his Lowell, Massachusetts mills.

But confiscating Confederate cotton and sending it North was just one way to make money. There were so many others.

There was no more cocaine. This would not do. It was a situation that must be rectified immediately. But she had such little energy. Not even enough to go to school. How many days had she missed now? Her head hurt so bad that she couldn't count. Maybe that was a good thing. At least the headaches kept her from school.

Clara noted, "Oh! I am so tired, so weary! So sick of school. I was up before six, and here I have been penning, ciphering, until my brains dizzy and every nerve seems to be deprived of its strength. I can imagine no life so happy as that one which is 'schoolless.' I am tired, yes heartily tired of studying. In fact it is too much for me. I shall sink under my many trials."[74]

Now that she had resolved to stay home, there was still the problem of procuring the cocaine. "Yesterday afternoon Alice and I went to the drugstore to pay the residue of the Cocaine."[75]

The clerk didn't have any change, but fortunately for Clara, he told her to pay another day. She was able to go home and relieve her aching head—that is, until her next headache.

Less than two months later, Clara Solomon was again searching the pharmacies for the precious drug. "The object of our expedition was to purchase some 'Cocaine', which is awfully needed by the 'whole family.'"

Lamentably, it began to rain. Clara and her sister decided to wait it out—the drug was desperately needed at home. Yet the weather did not cooperate, and the two sisters returned home empty-handed. "Another day and no 'Cocaine.'"[76]

Clara tried again the next day, but the pharmacist was out. He offered to make up a batch, and Clara agreed to pick it up the next day. "I am so sorry that we are departed of this excellent article. 'Oh thou art the cause of this sorrow Abe Lincoln.'" Finally, two days later, two days without the desperately needed pain reliever, Clara was able to procure some from a rival pharmacist: "It was more diminutive than Burnett's, but they say of a superior quality. I doubt it, and prefer 'our Cocaine.'"[77]

Nevertheless, Clara took what she had, and the pain went away. At least for a while.

May 2, 1862

The Yankees took possession of the St. Charles Hotel. Butler returned to his ship to retrieve his wife, Sarah. He hoped that she would be impressed with her new surroundings. She deserved the best and he believed he had procured it for her.

After breakfast, he summoned Mayor Monroe and other city representatives. The mayor refused to come until the guard told him, "You had better not have me deliver that message to General Butler, for if you do

I shall have to bring you to him in a way that may be unpleasant." Not long after, the mayor and his comrades sat at Butler's recently requisitioned table in the ladies' parlor on the first floor of the St. Charles Hotel.

Meanwhile, a large mob was forming outside the hotel on Common and St. Charles Streets. They were loud, obnoxious and offensive. Butler was unable to conduct the business at hand. When one of his officers, Lieutenant George De Kay, came into the parlor in a torn uniform asking for instructions, the general told him to clear the streets with artillery. Immediately, his secessionist guests leapt up and begged him to rescind the order. He replied, "Why this emotion, gentlemen? The cannon are not going to shoot our way, and I have borne this noise and confusion as long as I choose to."

The mayor begged to be allowed to quiet the crowd, but he failed to do so, as did the other secessionists.

Meanwhile, Butler stood off to the side, scanning the crowd. He saw one man in particular who caught his attention. The man stood below on the sidewalk, jeering with the mob while wearing a piece of a United States flag pinned to his shirt. Upon inquiry, Butler learned that it was William Mumford—the man who had torn down the U.S. flag over the Mint. The general told the officer next to him to get a good look at Mumford and be sure that he could identify him at a later date. Butler had plans for Mumford.[78]

The crowd grew more restive and the taunts became more aggressive. Finally, the general stepped forward. Almost immediately after, the requested battery came roaring down St. Charles. When the mob saw the cannon headed their way, they quickly surmised that the man they called "The Beast" would not hesitate to earn that sobriquet, and they quickly dispersed.

Butler returned to his desk and began flipping through a prodigious quantity of letters, most of them hate mail—veiled threats and taunts about his appearance, his head, his weight but mostly his eyes.

He then turned his attention to his unwilling guests. The general read a handful of the more colorful death threats and jibes to his audience: "Old Cock-eyed," "Lobster-eye," "Picayune." He then informed them that New Orleans was now under martial law. Former U.S. senator and ambassador to Spain and now spokesman for the New Orleans secessionists Pierre Soule promptly protested. He informed the general that the people of the Crescent City were gallant, honorable and would not hesitate to evict anyone who dared usurp their rights. He demanded that Butler withdraw his troops from the city or he, Soule, could not be

Benjamin Butler during the war years. *From Library of Congress.*

held responsible for the consequences. Considering that New Orleans had surrendered without a fight, these were empty—even foolish—words. Butler was quick to respond:

> *I did not expect to hear from Mr. Soule a threat in this occasion. I have long been accustomed to hear threats from southern gentlemen in political conventions; but let me assure gentlemen present, that the time for tactics of*

that nature has passed never to return. New Orleans is a conquered city. If not, why are we here? How did we get here? Have you opened your arms and bid us welcome? Are we here by your consent? Would you or would you not, expel us if you could? New Orleans has been conquered by the forces of the United States, and by the laws of all nations, lies subject to the will of the conquerors.[79]

The message was unequivocal: New Orleans now belonged to the United States. And by extension to Benjamin Butler.

The Beast would soon earn himself another nickname: Spoons. He was given this sobriquet when he allegedly stole two separate sets of silver spoons from conquered New Orleanians.

CLARA WAS DETERMINED TO resist the Yankee occupiers. But how? What could a young woman do to resist? Surely, she would find a way. She "endeavored to kill as few mosquitoes as possible. For two reasons, the first being that we should be polluted by being touched by 'Yankee blood', and secondly each one increased the number and aids in biting and tormenting them. I wonder how they like them!"[80]

Alice and Clara were closing up the school. Before they left, Clara wrote some anti-Union sentiment on the board, "hoping they would meet the eyes of some Yankee."[81]

They walked down Canal Street. Clara "'Made faces' at the Yanks I saw." When they walked by a Federal sentinel, Clara gathered up her skirt and put her handkerchief to her nose to avoid his noxious fumes. As she passed, she "made some vague allusions to the night air and yellow fever."[82]

But mostly she fumed and vented to her diary: "Old Butler! If he could only have as many ropes around his neck as there are ladies in the city and each have a pull! Or if we could fry him! Or give him many salt things to eat, and have water in sight, and he unable to attain it!"[83]

MAY 10, 1862

A loud screech or sneer pierced the air above. The general glanced up just in time to see a line of women at the very end of a 180-degree pirouette. At that second, their skirts were descending to cover their undergarments.

Butler blurted out for all to hear, "Those women evidently know which end of them looks the best."[84]

Days later, Admiral Farragut was on the receiving end of a barrage when a woman "inadvertently" tossed a loaded chamber pot with the perfect trajectory on the admiral and his aide as they walked through the Quarter.

When Butler heard of this latest affront, he wrote to a friend in Massachusetts, saying, "Every opprobrious epithet, every insulting question was made by these bejeweled, becrinolined [sic], and laced creatures calling themselves ladies, towards my officers and soldiers, from the windows of houses and in the street....I had arrested the men who hurrahed for Beauregard,—could I arrest the women?"[85]

The situation only deteriorated, with Southern women stepping and turning aside whenever a Yankee passed by, holding their noses as if an odorous stench hung about every Federal soldier, pouring the contents of their chamber pots on Union passersby and even spitting directly in the faces of their Northern conquerors. Picayune Butler was soon to metamorphosize into the Beast.

On May 15, 1862, General Butler issued his infamous "Woman's Order," Order No. 28. It stated "As the officers and soldiers of the United

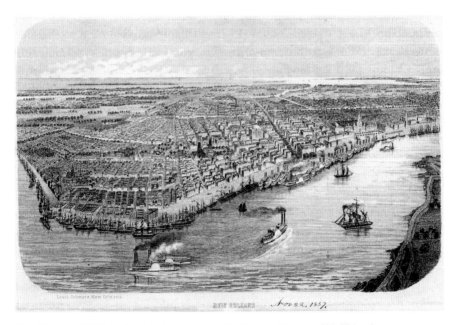

New Orleans in 1857, by Louis Schwartz. *From the Beinecke Library at Yale University.*

States have been subjected to repeated insults from the women (calling themselves ladies) of New Orleans, in return for the most scrupulous non-interference and courtesy on our part, it is ordered that hereafter when any female shall, by word, gesture, or movement, insult or show contempt for any officer or soldier of the United States, she shall be regarded and held liable to be treated as a woman of the town plying her avocation."

Benjamin Butler became the most hated man in the Confederacy. Jefferson Davis even went so far as to order the Yankee general be hanged upon capture. The French government banned the printing of his name. Great Britain filed complaints with Secretary of State Seward.

Benjamin Butler didn't care. His order would stand. So would the price on his head.

CLARA WALKED INTO A hornets' nest when she went to school on Friday, May 16. Her classmates were abuzz with General Butler's recent command—General Order No. 28. Her teacher silenced the students and proceeded to read the infamous order.

Clara simmered with rage. "And how did they expect to be treated. Can a woman, a Southern woman, come in contact with one of them and allow her countenance to retain its wonted composure. Will not the scornful feelings in our hearts there find utterance. They may control our actions, but looks, thy never can."[86]

MAY 30, 1862

The secessionists needed to be taught a lesson. A stern lesson.

The general never forgot a face. This skill enabled him to be a successful lawyer and politician. Now it would help him succeed in the realm of mob control.

He issued the warrant. Weeks later, he sat at his table-desk and wrote:

> *The defendant having been fully heard in his defence [sic], the Court upon full consideration pronounce him Guilty, and for sentence say that: Said William B. Mumford be hanged by the neck until dead—at or near the*

Mint in said City of New Orleans as such time as the Major General Commanding within this Department shall direct.

Let an order be made and Mumford be informed that he will be executed between the hours of 8 A.M. and 12 P.M. June 7, 1862.[87]

The designated day approached. The general had agreed to meet with the family of the man he planned to execute in two days. In fact, his carpenters were already constructing the gallows in front of the Mint where the execution was set to take place. The general intended for the condemned to hang at the very sight of his crime, with the Union flag that he had desecrated flapping in the wind above him.

Butler walked into the hotel parlor and called for the soon-to-be widowed and orphaned. He was greeted with a plea and a flood of tears. Mary Mumford begged for her husband's life. So did her three weeping children.

It was to no avail. Butler said he would not be swayed. He then asked a favor of the grieving wife: "Mumford believes he will not be executed. I wish you to convince him that he is mistaken. Whether I live or die he will die…. Let him in the few hours he has to live look to God for his pardon." He then sent the wailing family away.[88]

IN HER DIARY, CLARA wrote, "I had a most tantalizing dream last night in which I lavished upon 'Judo' the fondest caresses and kisses, and then awoke to find it but—a dream. But how I enjoyed them. Had they been genuine, my joy could not have been more intense."[89] She wanted a beau. Badly. As a sixteen-year-old girl approaching womanhood, she could think of little else. Along with drudging through her detestable lessons, it became her raison d'être.

She attended a military rally and was glad she did: "I am half in love with the handsome Capt. M. About 1 o'clock the procession commenced to pass and oh! the multitude of handsome, determined faces, and manly forms. I lost my heart over and over again, and as one fascinating creature would pass on, another would immediately fill his place. I had no idea that we had so many soldiers. How can we have any beaus!"[90]

For an adolescent, an object of affection could always be found. When the soldiers marched off to give the Yankees an overdue thrashing, she would turn her attention to the boys at home. "If such a thing as love at first sight is felt, I may safely say that I experienced, for I was fascinated by a gentleman in a splendid carriage, and not a soldier....I liked his face so much and when he drove off, and was lost to my view, oh! I felt so, so lonely and unhappy, and I know that we shall never meet again. In the crowd I searched in vain for him. His image is indelibly impressed on my mind."[91]

The search for a beau would go on, though the pool would soon drastically diminish.

June 7, 1862

Dr. William Mercer, octogenarian, secessionist, leading citizen and one of the few New Orleans citizens on civil terms with Butler, entered the general's parlor moments before the execution was to take place.

"O General, General, give me this man's life. I must soon go to meet my Maker; let me take with me that I have saved a fellow-creature's life. You can do it, you can do it."

"No, Doctor. The question is now to be settled whether law and order or a mob shall govern."

"Oh, no, General; a scratch of your pen will save him."

"True, Doctor, and a scratch of that same pen would put you in his place. My officers are loyal and true, and they won't question the reason of my order. They will obey first and question it, if at all, afterwards. Having this great power I must use it judiciously. I cannot."

The aged man left the general, tears pouring down his cheeks.[92]

The mob milled around the front of the Mint and all the way to the St. Charles Hotel. Everyone expected Mumford to be reprieved at the very last moment. Mumford, with the noose about his neck, looked down the street expecting to see an officer ride forth with the life-saving order.

At last, "the drop fell, and as it did there was a universal hush...and the crowd separated as quietly as if it were from the funeral of the most distinguished citizen."[93]

"THE ACCOUNT OF THE execution in Sunday's paper was enough to cast a gloom over the spirits of all, and I cannot think of the atrocious, inhuman crime, and suppress my tears. Universal sorrow seemed to pervade our community." Clara and Alice got little sewing done that night as they "sympathized with the poor widow and orphans."[94]

Fortunately, one of Alice's students dropped by for a visit and diverted some of Clara's gloom. Once the welcome visitor left, Clara returned her attention to her thimbles and thread, determined to make herself a new dress.

With the sorrow over the Mumford incident somewhat alleviated, a new dread filled her mind: impending examinations. Clara began to sew with even more diligence, delaying her own doom as long as she could.

———

BUTLER WAS CONDEMNED THROUGHOUT the Confederacy for the execution of Mumford. But open acts of hostility did cease in New Orleans. Of course, more clandestine forms of revolt continued. The general could deal with those people in a more humane way. Rather than execute them, he would send them to the hell that was Ship Island.

Soon secesh leaders, members of the press with Confederate sympathies and the wealthy who opposed Butler's policies were sent to the island prison. So were women who dared mock his authority. Butler understood the power of women. Lest he forget, he kept a permanent reminder in the form of a sign placed above his desk. It stated, "There is no difference between a He and a She Adder in their Venom." His infamous Woman Order illustrated his understanding of female power and his contempt for female secessionists. His treatment of Eugenia Levy Phillips showed that he intended to exorcise those of the "fairer sex" who were filled with venom.

———

IT WAS GRADUATION NIGHT, and Clara was determined to look her very best. "After dinner, I began making preparations, and after much thought decided on my pretty barege skirt, and ditto white body, and was some time in making my toilette, and when I had finished did not look quite as well as would have…Beauty [Phillips]. How discouraging!" Then again, Clara would never be able to compete with her idol. All she could do was emulate her and hope for her continued friendship.

It could be worse for her, she thought. True, she would never equal the beauty of Alice, and certainly not that of "Beauty," but at least she was passably pretty. And her sense of style and impeccable manners would lead her to eventually find the ideal husband. At least she was not as hopeless as some of her classmates. "Maggie and I enjoyed ourselves commenting upon the different girls, and pitying in particular poor Emma Lewis, who is so ugly."

And at least Clara still had better fingernails than Maggie.[95]

JUNE 1862

The coffin carrying the remains of Union lieutenant George De Kay was being carried through the streets. Mrs. Eugenia Levy Phillips was enjoying a children's party on her balcony. She loved children. She hated Yankees. Either through delight in the little ones or pleasure at the sight of the hearse, Eugenia burst into happy laughter. The Yankees took note and informed General Butler. When he learned that the culprit was a Jew and a friend of Confederate secretary of state Judah Benjamin, he ordered her arrest.

Eugenia was at home sewing and talking to her daughter, Fanny, when a Union officer arrived with a summons to appear before General Butler. She claimed that it must be a mistake, but the officer insisted. Then, Eugenia remembered having assisted in raising funds for the recently widowed wife of William Mumford. She calmed her panicked family and promised to return shortly. Surely the Beast would not punish her for aiding a widow.

Eugenia arrived at the customhouse and was brought before Butler. As a greeting, the general exclaimed, "You are seen laughing and mocking at the remains of a Federal officer. I do not call you a common woman of the town, but an uncommonly vulgar one, and I sentence you to Ship Island for the War."

The ardent secessionist replied, "I was in good spirits the day of the funeral." Her response and subsequent refusal to apologize sealed her fate. Butler wrote the order that condemned her to the sands of Ship Island, and Captain Stafford—the hangman of William Mumford—led Eugenia to prison to await her deportation.

Eugenia was allowed a tearful farewell with her husband and children before she boarded the ship for her island prison. One day later, she disembarked and stepped into the ankle-deep, scorching sand and felt the sweltering summer heat. Then came the insects. For the next three and a half months, the mosquitoes and gnats would ally to turn the uncovered parts of her body into a massive feeding ground.

Eugenia was moved to her small box of a room that was atop a pile of sand. As inhospitable as her cell looked, the exhausted woman quickly moved inside to escape the torment of the insects. The bugs were soon replaced with tormenting visions of the upcoming months. "Truly a fearful [way] to punish a woman and tear her from her family because she was enjoying herself with her young children."

The following morning brought no relief to Eugenia. "The sun rose, hours elapsed, to find us unwashed, unfed, unnoticed. Not a human being came near us, even to bring a drop of water. The question arose as to whether we were to be starved or treated as human beings. Noon came on to find me pretty ill for want of sustenance."

Finally, the commandant of Ship Island, General Neal Dow, arrived at Eugenia's cell. It wasn't sustenance that he brought. "He said I ought to be hung or made to work at breaking stones for the fort (an amusement Gen. Butler inaugurated for the rich men of New Orleans when they would not disgorge their riches to him) with a forty-lb. chain on my leg (saw this also every day), and indulging in various epithets too low for my pen to write."

After several hours passed, a cook arrived with Eugenia's rations. He served the same meal she would be dining on for the next three and a half months. "He scraped from the [plate] a mess of beans and spoiled beef, something which was yellow with saleratus, which he called bread, and another mess called tea."

After one month, Eugenia became ill with what was called "brain fever." The doctor prescribed "quiet." Her sentence continued, uncommuted. After nearly four months of exile, Eugenia received a note proclaiming, "Mrs. Phillips, imprisoned at Ship Island, is hereby released, in order to prevent the sufferings of the *wholly innocent*." She was furious.

How dare he insinuate she was in such a "condition"?[96] *And to send the implication through an officer!* Outraged, Eugenia briefly thought of objecting to her release based on such an insinuation, but in the end, common sense prevailed. The thought of seeing her family made her accept her release.

Eugenia Levy Phillips joyfully rejoined her family in New Orleans. It would not be long before the household relocated to Confederate Georgia for the remainder of the war.[97]

—⸱⸱—

CLARA READ OF EUGENIA'S incarceration in the evening newspaper. Eugenia's daughter was Beauty. Beauty had lost her mother because of the loathsome Beast. Clara seethed with empathetic indignation. That evening, she wrote in her diary:

The charge against her is "she is found on the balcony of her house during the passage of the funeral of De Kay, laughing and mocking at his remains, and upon being inquired of by Com. Gen. if this fact were so, contemptuously replies, 'I was in good spirits that day.'" This is one of the outrages of But. command separating this woman from her family and keeping her in confinement in that miserable place, no one knows how long. And what anyway could a woman's taunts do them![98]

Henceforth, Clara would have to tread carefully when offering her passive-aggressive resistance to the Yankee occupiers. She was quite certain that her frail constitution would struggle mightily against the climate of Ship Island.

FINALLY, PRESIDENT LINCOLN COULD no longer justify keeping such a hated man in charge of such an important city. Where there's smoke there's usually fire. And there were simply too many accusations of graft and corruption directed at Benjamin Butler. Lincoln respected his general's firm hand, and he needed his political support, but keeping the political general in New Orleans had become untenable. The Beast was officially replaced on December 12, 1862, by another inept political general: Nathaniel Banks.

Few were sad to see the Beast go.

A Confederate woman wrote the general as he prepared to depart:

Not content with thieving and stealing from all sorts and conditions of men, you insulted our best citizens, and used language to our gentlemen such as they never heard, and such as you only are capable of uttering….May you return to Lowell (the Yankee hole that gave you birth), and when your miserable wife decks herself off in her stolen finery, and appears with you in public, may every eye be turned, and every finger pointed to the "pair of Yankee thieves"….May the spirit of the glorious Mumford haunt you by night.
—*One of your She Adders*[99]

Even segments of the Yankee Press vilified the avaricious general. A writer for the *New Yorker* wrote an open letter to Butler:

You are to answer to the people of the North for your thieving; an account incoming out which may take down your bombastic vanity a degree, and another little account for which you try on all public occasions to excuse

*yourself, is the murder of Mumford, whom you call a drunken gambler,—
the idea of a drunken sot like you calling another a "drunken gambler"....
Your rotten-hearted carcass must be deprived of vitality, your thieving soul
of life, so prepare to meet your cohort, the Devil, who wants you more than
this country does.*[100]

While much of this venom directed at Butler—and his historical legacy—can be attributed to bitter secessionists who lost the war and political rivals in the North, several hard facts that question Butler's integrity refuse to go away. Butler biographer Chester G. Hearn summed up the general's New Orleans tenure: "[Butler's brother] Andrew came to New Orleans with little money. The general's capital consisted of about $150,000. By 1868 Butler was worth $3 million. Andrew then died that year, leaving his own considerable estate to the general. Butler's fortune could not have been amassed on a general's salary, dividends from stockholdings, legal fees, or his reentry into national politics. This leaves but one source to account for the swiftly amassed fortune—New Orleans."[101]

It is no wonder that New Orleanians never erected a statue in his honor. Although its most famous statue still bears the "Mark of the Beast."

CAPTURE OF NEW ORLEANS — FLEET PASSING FORTS ON THE MISSISSIPPI

Capture of New Orleans: The Fleet Passing Forts on the Mississippi. From the Beinecke Library at Yale University.

NEW ORLEANIANS ADORED ANDREW Jackson. The residents had a larger-than-life statue of him in the former Place d'Armes, now named Jackson Square. Had they forgotten that their beloved hero was not always so beloved in the city? He, too, had enforced martial law.[102] He, too, was regaled as an incorrigible tyrant. He, too, was considered a savior of his country.

The general decided to send a message. Butler had an inscription carved into the base of the beloved statue: "THE UNION SHALL AND MUST BE PRESERVED." Three decades earlier, Jackson had given toast in Washington, D.C., in which he exclaimed, "Our Federal Union: It must be preserved!" Butler knew that these sentiments (albeit spoken in a different context in 1830) would anger the secessionists who had been sending him threatening mail and giving him a difficult time.

In fact, his inscription was viewed by many in New Orleans as graffiti.

CLARA SOLOMON SURVIVED THE reign of Benjamin Butler. She graduated from the school she detested so much and found the beau she dreamed of so often…sort of.

In 1866, she married Julius Lilienthal, a respected Jewish jeweler twenty years her senior. Less than two years later, Clara was a twenty-two-year-old widow with no children. She moved in with her parents.

Five years later, she married the doctor who had treated her aged, sickly husband. Dr. George Lawrence and Clara had four daughters together and lived at least some of the time in New Orleans. When her second husband died in 1889, Clara and her three daughters moved to New Orleans, where they lived until Clara's death in 1907—forty-five years after her nemesis Benjamin Butler was forced to leave.[103]

Butler's reign in New Orleans was scandalous, effective and brief. He is now just a footnote in New Orleans history, forgotten by most residents. The Beast tried to subdue a population while enriching himself. And yet life went on. Clara and her contemporaries and young girls for the next century and a half continued to primp themselves, study for tests, fantasize about their weddings and pray for the perfect beau. And, of course, many women of the nineteenth, twentieth and twenty-first centuries actively engaged in politics, business and the arts. The half of the population General Butler loathed and feared made a far more lasting contribution to New Orleans.

In the end, it was the "venomous she-adders" who endured.

PIERCED WITH SLANDER'S VENOMED SPEAR

The Sad Tale of Cap Murphy and Recorder Ford

A cold wind blew, and Cap Murphy, coat buttoned to his neck, stared at the muck-filled canal. A pistol was tucked into his pocket, pressed against his hip. He thought he might need it—but not enough to keep it easily accessible. His coat blocked the pistol.

Cap Murphy sat on the steps of a lottery office with two friends that December afternoon in 1884, watching a gang of convicts toiling in Claiborne Canal. They were cleaning it. Murphy oversaw. That was his job, along with being a fireman. He sat in a sunny spot on the steps of a house with two other city employees. They talked softly about upcoming fire company elections. Murphy was marshal and was looking to get reelected.

A woman sat on the steps of the house next door. Another woman sat on the steps of the house across St. Philip Street. Witnesses.

One of Murphy's friends spotted a pair of men walking toward them on St. Philip, in the direction of the French Quarter. *Aren't those...Judge Ford's men?*

Murphy tracked the two men with his eyes. His adrenaline spiked and words flashed through his mind: *liar, coward, perjurer, poltroon.* His attention was fixed on the two men. He didn't see the other three rounding the corner of Claiborne Street behind him. One of the three was John Murphy, a policeman and cousin of Judge Ford's, who had sores on his neck and hands. Another was Pat Ford, the judge's brother. The third was Judge Ford himself. They had several revolvers between them, and the revolvers were pointed at Murphy.

The corner on Claiborne Avenue where Ford's men first confronted Cap Murphy, as seen in 2019. *From Josh Foreman.*

Gunshots.

Murphy's seatmate fell, struck across the chest. Murphy was jolted by the impact of a pistol ball cutting into his shoulder. Murphy jumped up and reached for his pistol. Stymied—the pistol sat behind a layer of heavy cloth. The prisoners who'd been cleaning the canal climbed out, glistening with slime, at the sound of the shots. The woman next door got inside quick.

A streetcar traveling down Claiborne happened to pass as the men opened fire, and passengers on the streetcar watched as the conflict unfolded.

Murphy ran toward the Quarter, still trying to get to his gun.[104]

FOR FIVE YEARS, CAP Murphy had been living on the rim of a whiskey tumbler. He should have been killed on a winter's night in 1879 at a bar he helped run—the Gaiety Theatre at the corner of Baronne and Common Streets.

The Gaiety Theatre was the kind of place nineteenth-century New Orleanians went to listen to singing, watch plays and dancing and hear impersonations. It was a popular and raucous establishment in the 1870s—

the "People's Favorite Resort," it called itself in newspaper ads. But it had fallen on hard times by 1879.[105]

Murphy was drinking—drunk, to be honest—in the Gaiety Theatre around 1:00 a.m. on a Thursday morning in January 1879. He was talking with one of the female performers. Another man, a ne'er-do-well named Ed Cooney, sidled up to Murphy and the woman, an act that apparently rankled Murphy. Murphy ordered Cooney away, but Cooney, who was also quite drunk, refused to leave. Murphy cursed him, and then hit him. Cooney produced a knife, which he plunged into Murphy's body twice. Cooney ran, leaving Murphy to die on the floor of the theater.

Newspapers announced the following day that Murphy's wounds were critical and that he was not expected to recover. But he didn't die. Within a year, Murphy was healed and getting into more trouble.[106]

Murphy's brush with death seemed to steel him rather than scare him away from drinking and fighting. For five years following his near-fatal wounding at the Gaiety Theatre, Murphy lived recklessly. Less than a year later, he was busted for election fraud. A couple of years after that, he found himself again at the center of a theater brawl—this time at the Park Theatre on Royal Street.[107] News of his drinking and the disturbances that followed did not always make the paper, but he was arrested often.[108]

Of course, life was not all drinking and fighting and trouble for Cap. He was tall, fair-skinned and good-looking, a man in his early thirties and unencumbered by a wife, children and the responsibilities that come with a family.[109] Instead of a family, he had community. He had great friends at the fire station. They'd named a horse after him.[110] He had taken up the new sport of baseball a few years before and played on a club team that also bore his name.[111] He boxed, sometimes fighting in amateur matches.[112] He was free to work and spend nights drinking in the bars of the French Quarter (his favorite street was Royal).

Murphy also found camaraderie in political circles. He had come of age during a transitional time—Democrats had regained control of Louisiana in 1877, and federal troops had withdrawn from the state. Murphy was a Democrat and helped organize a "campaign club" in 1880 to support the campaign of General Winfield Scott Hancock, a Union hero from the Battle of Gettysburg, for president. Murphy served as the club's marshal. The club had a rather martial name—the E. John Ellis Guards—reflecting, perhaps, the members' willingness to fight.[113]

During the Reconstruction period, New Orleans had become a place where, as one historian put it, "Every conceivable source of graft was thoroughly explored." Prostitution was endorsed and supported by politicians and policemen on the take. The return of Louisiana to Democratic control did not eradicate political corruption; in fact, nothing changed.

By the late 1870s, as Murphy was getting interested in politics, New Orleans was "overrun" with corrupt politicians. The same historian wrote that "the payrolls of all departments were padded with the names of hoodlums and 'shoulder-hitters,' who were thus paid by the city for their labors as henchmen of the politicians." Another editorial put the problem in numerical terms: "Nowadays…nine-tenths of the criminals arrested for drunkenness and disorderly conduct are city employees."[114]

Though Murphy's drinking had brought him close to death on at least one occasion, for a while it did not land him in serious legal trouble. Murphy knew a judge in the New Orleans legal system, Thomas J. Ford, a friend from childhood who always saved Murphy's skin. Murphy would get drunk and get arrested. Then, as one account put it, "All that it was necessary for him to do was to send word to Judge Ford, and his release would be ordered at once."[115]

New Orleans, 1878–79. *From the Beinecke Library at Yale University.*

Murphy's frequent transgressions began to strain Judge Ford's willingness to help, though. The judge grew reluctant to order Murphy's release. Murphy's friends had to beg the judge to help Murphy. Judge Ford demanded that Murphy show up in his private office at the courthouse for a lecture. When the arrests didn't stop, Ford eventually began arraigning Murphy like anyone else, charging him twenty-five or thirty dollars for his release. Finally, Judge Ford's patience failed, and he ordered his once-friend to be sent to prison.[116]

The final push that would tip the two men's souring relationship into a full-blown feud came in October 1884, when Murphy was arrested for "insult, abuse, threats, and disturbing the peace." He came before Judge Ford, who not only fined him but *defined* him. In a note in the margins of his public record book, Ford wrote that Murphy was a "hoodlum, deadbeat, and city official." The public insult drove Murphy mad, and as one account put it, he "declared open and unrelenting war upon Ford."[117]

Murphy began bad-mouthing and threatening Judge Ford in public, and word soon reached Ford, who frequented Royal Street the same as Murphy. News of the two men's hatred spread throughout the community, and many thought the two would end up shooting each other in a Royal Street saloon. Lacking a public record book in which to insult Judge Ford, Murphy decided instead to post placards around town calling Ford "a liar, a coward, a perjurer, a poltroon, and a man without honor."[118]

Murphy was arrested for libel after posting the placards and was scheduled to be tried the following month, but an unrelated murder case pushed Murphy's trial back indefinitely. The public insult was apparently too much for Judge Ford to bear—he could not wait for the legal system, of which he was a representative, to deliver justice.

⌒—···—⌒

CAP MURPHY, FUMBLING WITH the buttons of his coat, ran toward Claiborne Street from the steps where he'd been sitting when he was ambushed. The two men he'd initially spotted walking down St. Philip were coming his way, but the three men who'd shot at him were still standing on the downtown side of Claiborne. Murphy was caught between the two groups.

When he reached the intersection of St. Philip and Claiborne, he finally freed his revolver. His pistol was the iconic revolver of the Old West—a Colt Single Action Army, a wildly popular gun among soldiers and civilians that

"Peacemaker" Colt Single-Action Army Revolver, serial no. 4519, 1874. *From Metropolitan Museum of Art.*

soon accumulated multiple nicknames, including "The Gun That Won the West" and "Peacemaker."[119] Murphy had six bullets, and there were five men coming toward him from two different directions. He fired at one group, then turned and fired at the other. He fired again and again and again. He fired five shots in total, leaving one bullet in the pistol, either by accident or because the bullet was defective. Nerves got the best of him though, and none of his bullets hit their marks.

With one bullet left, he shoved his revolver into his coat pocket and began running down Claiborne toward Dumaine Street. He ran across one of the prisoners he'd been supervising, who had climbed out of the canal and onto the sidewalk when the shooting started. The prisoner asked for Murphy's pistol and told him he'd cover him while Murphy escaped. Murphy stopped, pulled the pistol out, hesitating, thinking of some way this might work out for him. He decided giving the prisoner his revolver would be futile and continued his flight. The moment's hesitation had allowed his pursuers to gain on him, though.

His pursuers continued chasing him down Claiborne and again shot at him as he ran. Two of the bullets fired at Murphy had struck by that point— one grazing his left shoulder and another shattering his right. Seriously wounded, Murphy reached Dumaine and turned down the street, running toward the Quarter.

One of the men pursuing Murphy stopped at the corner of Dumaine and Claiborne, rested his pistol on the side of a house, took aim at

The spot where Cap Murphy fell to the street and died, as seen in 2019. *From Josh Foreman.*

Murphy and fired. The assassin's bullet entered Murphy's back and passed through a lung and an artery before lodging in his breastplate. Murphy turned, took a last look at his pistol and fell, his cheek pressed against Dumaine Street, already dead or with seconds left to live. One of the assassins stepped to his body, brought his revolver close enough to Murphy's face that the ensuing discharge would burn the dead man's skin and fired two more shots—one into his cheek and one into his neck— then fled up Robertson Street.[120]

IN MANY WAYS, CAP Murphy and Thomas J. Ford had followed similar trajectories. They were about the same age, involved in New Orleans politics and baseball players. Ford was a handsome young man, a dapper dresser who wore a sweeping handlebar mustache and a pronounced part in his wavy hair. They were both firemen, and both served as marshal of their respective fire precincts. Both men even had firehouse horses named after them. Both came from Irish heritage, though Murphy was a bit further removed from his; Murphy's parents had been born in the American South, whereas Ford's parents were both Irish immigrants.[121]

The two men were very different too. Ford was a married man with a devoted wife and several children, whereas Murphy was a bachelor. Murphy sat many times in front of a judge's bench after his drunken blowouts. Ford was the man sitting on the other side of the bench, passing judgment, literally, on New Orleanians who'd run afoul of the law.

Still, Judge Ford showed, from time to time, that he was not afraid of a fight or of resorting to violence to settle a dispute. Murphy was not the only man with whom Ford had feuded. In an episode eerily similar to the one that would follow in 1884, Judge Ford found himself "placarded" by another disgruntled city employee in 1883.

That incident stemmed from a disagreement between Judge Ford and a police detective named T.J. Boasso. Boasso had arrested another man for "being a dangerous character." The man had gone before Judge Ford, who freed him. Boasso didn't agree with the judge's decision and confronted Ford in the judge's private chambers. Whatever was said behind closed doors led Ford to hit Boasso. A third party burst into the chambers and broke up the fight.

New Orleans, 1878–79. *From the Beinecke Library at Yale University.*

Boasso left the courthouse, but the row between him and the judge was inflamed by chatter on the streets of New Orleans. The judge had apparently insulted Boasso—a grievance that could not go ignored.

Boasso decided to take revenge on Ford in a way Murphy would emulate a year later: Boasso had placards made up accusing Ford of being a despicable character. The placards read:

To whom it may concern:

I hereby brand
Thomas J. Ford as
A Liar,
A Coward, and
A Poltroon. T.J. Boasso[122]

Boasso was arrested for libel. As in the Murphy incident, Boasso's trial was postponed indefinitely. Judge Ford wielded the power of the law but couldn't seem to adequately punish his libelous enemies.[123]

———··——

AS NEWS OF CAP Murphy's murder spread through the city, friends of the slain man made their way toward a house on Fulton Street. Murphy's body had been autopsied and moved to that house—his mother's house. Hundreds came to pay their respects that first night.

Murphy's funeral was scheduled for the following day, and his friends from the fire company showed up in their carriages hours beforehand. Murphy's mother and siblings cried beside his casket as a preacher from Felicity Street Methodist Church preached. Murphy's body was transported to Odd Fellows' Rest, an above-ground cemetery, and was carried by firemen to a vault, where it was placed.

Murphy's murder had taken place in the heart of New Orleans in the middle of the afternoon. Many witnessed the events, including the passengers of the streetcar that passed at the time gunfire erupted. The men responsible for Murphy's murder were arrested almost immediately. Six of them were charged with murder, including Judge Ford, his brother Pat and John Murphy, the policeman with the rash on his hands and neck.[124]

The *Daily Picayune* was aghast at the brazen murder and sounded alarms on its editorial page. "The hand of the assassin," the paper wrote, "is no longer gloved." The *Picayune* wrote that New Orleans had become a "Carnival of Blood" where murder was not perpetrated by outcasts under cover of night but by "officers of the law" whose job it was to punish crime and preserve peace. The murder of Cap Murphy was an affront to New Orleanians' peace of mind and sense of security—to the city's sense of civilization itself. In an understated but poignant jab at Judge Ford and his co-conspirators, the paper published that "the gentlemen who murdered Murphy should not feel hurt if they are called hoodlums."[125]

The *Picayune*'s reporting in the days that followed the murder give a sense of the public outrage that the murder stirred up. The murder of a well-liked young man created "extraordinary excitement and indignation" in the city, and the newspaper did not blame the city's residents for their outrage. The six men accused of murder, the paper wrote, were lucky they had not been lynched by a mob—a punishment the equal of the "absolute contempt for the law" the murderers themselves had shown.[126]

People felt particularly betrayed by Judge Ford, whom the city of New Orleans "almost universally" held responsible for the murder prior to any trial. It had been Ford's "particular duty to vindicate the law," the *Picayune* wrote, and he had turned to assassination to end his feud with Murphy.[127]

As preparations were made to try the six (plus two others arrested later) in the weeks following the murder, New Orleanians paid close attention, hoping that their faith in the city's justice system could be restored with a fair, thorough trial and an appropriate punishment. The Ford trial would be a referendum on the justice system itself. Not everyone was optimistic that justice would prevail; in an editorial, the *Democrat* of Alexandria, Louisiana, predicted the men's trial would "end in a grand fizzle." In nose-thumbing fashion, the editorial went on to blame the people of New Orleans for allowing lawlessness to continue in the city.[128]

Faith in the integrity of the justice system was not helped by reports of witness tampering taking place inside and outside the city jail. In one brazen episode, two policemen marched the four witnesses who'd been cleaning Claiborne Canal when the shooting erupted from the city prison to the parish prison, where Judge Ford and the other accused were being kept. The witnesses were ushered to a side chamber of the jail where they were brought before Judge Ford and asked whether they'd seen the judge at the shooting. They had not, they said. Then the canal cleaners were brought into the jailhouse yard, where the other five accused murderers stood. They were asked by Judge Ford whether they had seen *any* of the men present at the murder. Again, they answered that they had not.[129]

A collage of three of the killers of Cap Murphy, based on sketches of the men that accompanied a March 13, 1886 story in the *New Orleans Times Democrat*. (*From left:*) Thomas J. Ford, John Murphy and Pat Ford. *From Josh Foreman.*

When the accused finally came to trial, people from the city packed the courtrooms. Initial testimony indicated that the accused were most certainly responsible for Murphy's murder. Judge Ford maintained that he was not present at any time during the fracas, despite testimony from several witnesses to the contrary.[130]

The trial went on for more than a week. Then the public's hopes for a fair trial were cracked like a pecan shell—a policeman found a secret letter in a pile of laundry. It was a letter that one of the jurors, George Runte, had written to his wife.

The letter revealed that eleven of the twelve jurors wanted to find John Murphy and Pat Ford guilty of manslaughter and to set the other accused—including Judge Ford—free. A lone black man wanted to vote for a guilty verdict, and the author of the letter expressed his intention to push for a mistrial, because "we will not have a negro man to have the pleasure of saying that we had to come with him." The letter writer also confessed to being secretly in touch with Judge Ford, asked his wife to send newspaper clippings of the trial (along with fresh laundry) and revealed that his wife had previously begged him through another letter to "save Mrs. Ford's husband."[131]

When news of the secret letter came out, the judge in the case declared a mistrial and discharged the jury. Runte and another juror were imprisoned following the fiasco, and another four jurors were indicted for perjury.[132]

A new trial was held almost immediately with a completely new jury. This time, the jury did decide to convict. Pat Ford, the brother of Judge Ford, and John Murphy, the policeman with the rash on his neck and hands, were convicted of murder and sentenced to be hanged. Judge Ford and the two other men on trial were convicted of manslaughter and sentenced to twenty years of hard labor at the state penitentiary. Judge Ford resigned his judgeship upon hearing the verdict.[133]

IN MARCH 1895, THOMAS J. Ford stepped from the gates of the Louisiana State Penitentiary wearing a suit and black derby. He had spent ten years laboring as a convict. His wife was there to meet him that day. In fact, her diligent lobbying had led to his pardon ten years before his sentence was supposed to finish.[134]

Judge Ford had spent his ten years at the penitentiary in Baton Rouge, seemingly trying to prove that he was one of the good guys—as part of his pardon application, powerful friends in the state government, including the attorney general and lieutenant governor, vouched for his service as a prisoner. He had rescued female inmates when fire broke out, cared for the injured when a tornado hit, ratted on his fellow inmates when they were plotting an insurrection and alerted guards of other prisoners' plans of escape.[135]

The officials' letters to the governor, who had to sign the pardon for it to take effect, even cast serious doubt on Judge Ford's initial involvement in the murders. Yes, Attorney General M.J. Cunningham wrote, Ford was probably the instigator of the murders, but several people have sworn since the trial that Judge Ford was actually at his fire company's engine house at the time of the fracas on the street.[136]

Judge Ford restarted his life after being released from prison, helping to raise his children into adulthood and getting back into the legal profession—this time as a lawyer. He lived another twenty-two years after being released from prison. The report of his death in 1917 noted that he had been prominent in city politics in the 1880s but made no mention of his feud with Murphy and the subsequent imprisonment.

Cap Murphy and Tom Ford, like two towering oak trees struggling to shade each other out, had caused one another's destruction, as well as the destruction of many around them. Murphy was cut down during his prime, of course. Pat Ford and John Murphy were hanged, and the two men convicted of manslaughter alongside Judge Ford had been worked to death at the state penitentiary. Judge Ford had lost ten years of his life and his once-promising career. Murphy and Ford had proved the old verse, "Whoever sheds the blood of man, by man his blood will be shed."

At the root of all the bloodshed and recklessness was hubris—Cap Murphy, since surviving a stabbing in a New Orleans theater, thought nothing could kill him. Judge Ford, rising on the currents of city power, thought he was above the law. The two men clashed and neither backed down. The hemoclysm that followed shocked New Orleans and proved to doubting citizens that justice could actually be done.

6

LIBERIA OR BUST

Robert Charles Versus New Orleans

A passerby alerted the three police officers. Two suspicious men—black men—had been sitting on a stoop conversing quietly. What were they up to? Because they were black, the passerby could think of only a few answers. Gambling illegally, scoping out a house to rob, or—a favorite of the New Orleans Police Department—being "a dangerous and suspicious character." The last option allowed the police to keep the suspect behind bars for a few weeks "without having to worry about the niceties of evidence."[137] Regardless, the passerby thought they were up to no good. They must be—they were black.

One of the two men, Robert Charles, was one of the few willing and able to do something about the injustice he saw all around him. He carried a pistol. But the weapon was not as dangerous to the white establishment as was his mind.

Charles had come to the conclusion that the white and black races could not coexist. Consequently, he planned to take as many people as he could to the recently established nation of Liberia. He began to distribute literature regarding the refuge of ex-slaves.

When the dust finally settled in that summer of 1900, white New Orleans would come to see Charles's work with the Liberia movement differently. A reporter for the *Times-Democrat* explained that Charles's interest in Liberia coincided with his "descent into evil," stating, "In the course of time Charles developed into a fanatic on the subject of Negro oppression and neglected business to indulge in wild tirades whenever he could find a listener. He

Illustration based on a sketch of Robert Charles that appeared in the *Times-Democrat* on July 25, 1900. *From Josh Foreman.*

became more anxious to make converts than to obtain subscribers, and the more conservative drakes began to get afraid of him. Meanwhile he got into touch with certain agitators in the North and made himself a distributing agent for their literature."[138]

Many people in the white New Orleans establishment saw black New Orleanians as a problem, yet when a black man began to recruit black people to immigrate to Africa, he was labeled a dangerous fanatic.

The policemen found Charles and his friend Leonard Pierce sitting on the front steps of 2815 Dryades Street on July 23. Charles and Pierce had been waiting on two young black women who lived nearby. The women were renting the back rooms of the Uptown house from a white lady. It was 11:00 p.m., and there was no way the white lady was going to admit two black men into the house. Or at any time for that matter. So, Charles and Pierce waited until the front lights went out.

Then the police arrived.

Their arrival did not bode well for the two men. True, they had just been sitting on a stoop. True, they roomed together in a house only a few squares away on Fourth Street. True, they had not committed a crime. But it was nearly midnight. They were unemployed. And they were black.

Unbeknownst to the three police officers, one was also armed.[139]

⌐─··─⌐

THE IDEA OF SENDING free blacks to Africa caught on in the United States in the early 1800s. Paul Cuffe, a rich black New Englander, was taken by the idea and personally transported some free blacks to Sierra Leone. Cuffe saw Africa as a place where a new civilization could take root—one that rewarded character, not skin color. President Thomas Jefferson was a proponent of the idea, but some whites favored sending free blacks—of whom there were about 319,000 in the United States in 1830—to Africa for less altruistic reasons. Jefferson also saw the idea as a preventative measure to the mixing of the races. Other whites thought it was a good idea to send free blacks as far away from their enslaved brethren as possible to quash any support of insurrection. Some believed slave owners would be more likely to free their slaves if they knew there was a colony for them in Africa, while others thought the idea was a good way to spread Christianity.[140]

The organization that actually got the ball rolling on colonization was the American Colonization Society, founded in 1816. The organization was started by whites, including some prominent people such as Francis Scott Key, Henry Clay and the president of the University of Georgia, Reverend Robert Finley. The group was procolonization but not abolitionist, and some of the members of the group actually owned slaves. In addition, its vision of a colony in Africa was of black colonists ruled by white leaders.

The idea caught on with President James Monroe, who saw a colony for free blacks as a place where the United States could ship victims of the newly outlawed international slave trade who were captured at sea. Monroe offered to provide the colonists with enough supplies to get started in Africa, and in 1820, the first of the American Colonization Society's ships sailed for Africa carrying eighty-eight free blacks. Two years later, the colonists (those who survived, that is—yellow fever ravaged many) claimed Liberia on the west coast of Africa, south of Sierra Leone, as a U.S. colony.[141]

With the colony established, free blacks from across the United States began looking across the Atlantic at a potential new home. New Orleans was a natural port of departure for free blacks in Mississippi, like the seventy-one who boarded the *Rover* in 1835 and set sail for the colony.[142]

Finley, the university president who helped found the American Colonization Society and had been living in Liberia, recruited passengers for the *Rover* himself. Three of the passengers were native New Orleaneans, but the rest were from Mississippi. Their stories illustrate the cruelty in the lives they sought to escape. Hard choices and broken families were the norm.

Archy Moore was one passenger trying to leave a cruel life behind. A free black man from Mississippi, Archy Moore was a Methodist who had visited Liberia once in 1832. He was impressed with the colony, where healthy and religious colonists were making their livings growing corn, rice, sugar cane and a host of tropical crops. "There alone can the black man enjoy true freedom," he wrote upon return. "And where their freedom is, shall be our country."[143]

He was working on buying the rest of his family's freedom in 1835. He paid nearly $1,800 for a son and daughter's freedom, but the rest of his family remained in bondage. When Finley notified him that the *Rover* would soon set sail from New Orleans, he jumped at the chance for a new life for himself and part of his family.[144]

Thatched roof buildings inside wooden fence in foreground, with church and houses in background—Cavalla, Liberia, 1877. *From Library of Congress.*

Moore's brother David also left on the *Rover*. David Moore had been a slave but had been emancipated for "meritorious service" nine years before. He was passionate about the idea of moving to Liberia. A successful farmer, David Moore paid more than $4,000 to buy the freedom of his wife, a female friend, six children and three grandchildren. David Moore loaded not only his family onto the *Rover* but also a cotton gin and $5,000 worth of tools, trade goods and cash.

Another of the passengers was Gloster Simpson, a free black Methodist minister whose wife and five children were slaves. The owner of Simpson's wife and children agreed to set them free so they could emigrate with Simpson. But there was a problem: the woman and her five children had been leased to another planter for a term of years. They ended up working for several more years, with Simpson waiting patiently for their time to be up. When it finally was, he booked their spot on the *Rover*.

The *Rover* arrived in Liberia the following month. Its passengers disembarked for life in the towns of Monrovia and Millsburg. But as more and more free black Mississippians headed for New Orleans and then Liberia in the following years, a new colony within the colony was established that drew them together: Mississippi in Africa.[145]

THE POLICE WANTED TO know what the two men were doing. After explaining that they were waiting for a friend, Robert Charles stood up abruptly. Patrolman August Mora later gave his version of what happened on Dryades Street: "I grabbed him. The Negro pulled, but I held fast, and he finally pulled me into the street. Here I began using my billet and the Negro jerked from my grasp and ran."

As Charles ran, he and Mora began shooting at each other. Officer Joseph Cantrelle also drew his pistol and began firing at Charles. The lone unarmed man, Leonard Pierce, sat terrified, frozen on the steps, with Officer Jules Aucoin's revolver pointed at his head.

Two bullets found their marks—one from Charles's pistol and one from Mora's. Mora fell to the banquette, blood pouring from his hip. Cantrelle took up the chase, running after the culprit and firing at him as he fled. Robert Charles, with a bullet in his thigh, ran as fast as he could through the Uptown streets of New Orleans.[146]

Charles ran down several banquettes, dripping blood as he did. He then doubled back and returned home. He prayed that Pierce had remained loyal—that he hadn't told the police the location of their apartment. Charles walked down the narrow alley to his door and realized that Pierce hadn't talked, at least thus far. The apartment was empty. Charles found the .38 Winchester rifle he had stashed there and waited.

Four hours later, at around three in the morning, a police wagon pulled up. They had figured out Charles might be hiding out at the address. Seven officers emerged. Four of them walked down the dark alley where six doors opened into six one-room apartments. The four patrolmen approached room number four and found the door slightly ajar. Captain Day pushed the door open and found a Winchester .38 pointed at his chest. A second later, it flashed and thundered in the darkness. Captain Day whirled around and fell dead on the walkway. Charles fired several more bullets into his corpse for good measure. Then, he lifted the rifle and fired a shot into the skull of another of the three stunned officers. He, too, fell to the walkway dead.

The other two patrolmen, including Jules Aucoin, finally pulled their pistols and began to return fire. By then, Charles had slammed his door shut and reloaded his rifle. The two officers ran into an adjacent room and hid. Charles emerged from his apartment and paced back and forth down the alley, daring the officers to come out and face him. They didn't.

Astonishingly, the three officers at the wagon also did nothing. For thirty minutes they simply waited for their captain and comrades to return from the alley, despite presumably hearing all of the gunshots.

One hour after the first shot was fired, Charles appeared instead. Standing at the entrance of the alley, he raised his rifle and fired a single shot at an officer standing by the wagon. He missed, but the shot sent all three running for safety.

Two hours later, at around five in the morning, Aucoin and his partner, Corporal Trenchard, emerged from their hiding place. By now, there was a small army of cops gathered outside the alley. But their target was no longer around. He was on the run with his pistol and death-dealing Winchester.

He had left behind his Liberia literature—his dream of immigrating to the country seemed to be slipping further and further away.[147]

ROVER WAS THE FIRST ship to carry free black Mississippians from New Orleans to Liberia, but it wouldn't be the last. Other ships departed New Orleans in the following years—the *Nehemiah Rich*, the *Laura* and the *Lime Rock*, to name a few. Within two decades, more than 1,500 settlers had made it to Mississippi in Africa, which had been absorbed by Liberia in 1841. Between 1821 and 1867, the American Colonization Society would transport some 13,000 settlers to Liberia.

In Liberia, settlers found a land that lacked many of the basic necessities, such as tools and feather beds, that had been available in the United States. What they found, instead, was a profusion of diseases that hadn't been present in their old home. Within a year or two of arriving, half of the settlers died of fever and disease. Settlers were crowded into small huts, sometimes ten to a hut, which facilitated the spread of disease.[148]

Settlers described Liberia as a place where "we have to live by the sweat of the brow for everything is scare and high." Some of those who emigrated were literate and could make a living in international trade and commerce, facilitating trade between the United States and Liberia. But most were illiterate and found themselves making their livings from agriculture. They grew cocoa, coffee, rice, cotton, sweet potatoes, cassava, collard greens, cabbage, eggplant and okra. The most successful settlers built plantation houses that were reminiscent of the U.S. South and farmed with a staff of servants and laborers made up of native Africans.[149]

Settlers often clashed with the Africans who had been living on the land prior to colonization. Most of the settlers had no real ethnic or historical connection to that part of Africa. Their memories were of the rural South, and they found themselves taking up the "mantle of command and aristocracy" in Liberia, as one historian put it. Sometimes, the relationship devolved into outright war. Native Africans were exploited as laborers in a system that resembled the slavery of the United States.[150]

By 1900, Liberia had established itself as an alternative to life in the United States for free blacks. It was still undeveloped and still a hard place to live, but it was there as an option. Liberia was the realization of a dream and the product of an experiment. It was there for people like Robert Charles, who saw it as a place where black men and women could govern themselves.

⌐—···—⌐

BY MIDDAY JULY 24, the largest manhunt in New Orleans history was underway. It seemed as if all of white New Orleans turned out to capture the black racial agitator and now murderer. The *Times-Democrat* reported, "Two blacks, who are desperate men, and no doubt will be proven burglars, made it interesting and dangerous for three bluecoats on Dryades street, between Washington Avenue and Sixth Street, the Negroes using pistols first and dropping Patrolman Mora. But the desperate drakes did not go free, for the taller of the two, Robinson [an alias used by Robert Charles], is badly wounded, while Leonard Pierce is in jail."[151]

The *Times-Picayune* printed Mayor Paul Capdevielle's proclamation:

$250 REWARD
Under the authority vested in me by law, I hereby offer, in the name of the city of New Orleans, $250 reward for the capture and delivery, dead or alive, to the authorities of this city, the body of the Negro murderer,
ROBERT CHARLES,
who, on Tuesday morning, July 24, shot and killed Police Captain John T. Day and Patrolman Peter J. Lamb, and wounded Patrolman August T. Mora.
PAUL CAPDEVIELLE, Mayor[152]

Despite the reward and promise of glory for bringing down "one of the most formidable monsters that has ever been loose upon the community," Charles could not be found. The police and mob became increasingly frustrated, and they turned that frustration on those who they believed were aiding and abetting the fiend: the black community.

A mob gathered near Lee Circle, where the mayor of Kenner, Louisiana, said in no uncertain terms that the citizens of New Orleans should resort to violence to punish black New Orleaneans for Charles's crimes:

I am from Kenner, gentlemen, and I have come down to New Orleans tonight to assist you in teaching the blacks a lesson. I have killed a Negro before, and in revenge of the wrong wrought upon you and yours, I am willing to kill again. The only way you can teach these Niggers a lesson and put them in their place is to go out and lynch a few of them as an object lesson. String up a few of them, and the others will trouble you no more. That is the only thing to do—kill them, string them up, lynch them! I will lead you, if you will but follow. On to the Parish Prison and lynch Pierce![153]

Fortunately for Leonard Pierce, the police defended the jail from the mob. Pierce was not lynched that evening. Twenty-eight other black people were not so lucky. Two mob murders are representative of the attacks that occurred on the night of July 26.

Seventy-five-year-old Baptiste Philo was on his way to work at the French Market. He heard a large, boisterous crowd in the distance, but he was simply an old man on his way to work to fulfill his duties as a second-class citizen. He continued on his way. It would prove a fatal decision. One hour

Mardi Gras *optocht* in New Orleans, circa 1883–93. *From Rijksmuseum.*

later, he was lying in a bed at Charity Hospital with a bullet in his abdomen. The doctors informed him that the wound was fatal.[154]

Another black man was chased onto a streetcar by a pursuing mob. He thought the car would be a refuge—that it would carry him away from the deadly mob. The mob surrounded the vehicle, forcing the conductor to put the brakes on.

"Get out, fellows," the mob leader yelled to the white men in the car. "All whites fall out."

The doomed black man knew what would come next. He tried hiding under a seat but was easily spotted. Several armed white men entered the car and dragged him out. He was struck with a club but was able to stay on his feet and took off running toward Canal Street. He didn't make it very far. More blows followed. Again, he tried to escape, but this time he fell into the gutter. As soon as he stood up, a bullet tore into his body and he fell again. He tried to rise a second time but was greeted with a volley of lead. He would not rise again.

The streetcar was allowed to continue down the line. The black man was never identified and was buried in a potter's field.[155]

FOURTEEN BLOCKS AWAY FROM his home on Fourth Street—where he had killed his first two victims—Robert Charles was preparing to fight it out. If it came to that. He was in a small room at 1208 Saratoga Street, with pistol and rifle in hand.

It took police three days to close in on the man. On Friday, July 27, Charles watched out the window as a police wagon pulled up and four officers stepped out. Corporal John Lally and Sergeant Gabriel Porteus began searching the premises. The latter caught sight of a water bucket and walked inside to get a drink. Charles was a few feet away in a closet. As soon as Porteus grabbed the dipper, Charles fired point blank into his chest. He then whipped the gun around on Lally and shot him in the gut.

Charles, now the killer of four policemen, ran upstairs. He knocked a hole in the wall, giving him access to the neighboring room. Over the next several hours he would dart back and forth between the two rooms, keeping an eye on the courtyard and both flanking alleys.

As a crowd gathered and more and more police arrived, Charles quietly stuck his gun out of the window, spotted a nineteen-year-old white man leaning against a fence and fired. The young man, Arthur Brumfield, fell

THE BLACK HUNTER.

The Black Hunter from *Century Magazine*, April 1886. *From Internet Archive.*

to the ground with a bullet in his hip. The crowd around him dispersed in a panic. Arthur tried to do the same, crawling along the now bloodied dust. He looked back, caught sight of the rifle still aimed at him and screamed, "For God's sake, don't shoot!" A bullet through his chest made those his final words.

Within the hour, more than ten thousand people were at, near or on their way to Saratoga Street. Mayor Capdevielle ordered the state militia to the scene in case the mob turned its fury on the black population.

Surrounded on all sides, Charles continued to dash from room to room, occasionally rising to fire into the crowds. Whenever he did so, scores of shots returned his fire. Soon all the windows were busted out and the house's facade was pockmarked with bullets.

Arthur Brumfield, one of Charles's victims, based on a sketch from the *Times-Democrat*, July 31, 1900. *From Josh Foreman.*

Still, Charles continued his hopeless defense. He critically wounded another seven officers and vigilantes and slightly injured another dozen.

But Charles only had so many bullets. And the crowd only had so much patience.

Eventually, Captain William King realized that exchanging bullets with Charles was becoming too high of a cost. King and some helpers snuck into the downstairs room and lit a mattress on fire before running back out. Five minutes later, 1208 Saratoga Street was engulfed in smoke and flames. For a brief period, Charles continued to dart from room to room, firing occasionally. Then all was quiet. Too quiet.

The desperado emerged from the front door, hat low on his forehead and Winchester raised to shoulder height. Before anyone realized what was happening, he sprinted across the yard toward the front door of a new house, 1210 Saratoga Street.

As Charles burst into the entrance, a bullet sent him to the ground. He rolled over, intending to return fire, but dozens of bullets tore into his body. And then dozens more. As more and more people ran to the firing, they, too, emptied their guns into the corpse. And still more came. More bullets. More and more and more. Soon, little remained of the man who had terrorized New Orleans for several days. Nevertheless, Captain Trenchard—who had hidden with fellow officer Jules Aucoin in a dark room after Charles shot Captain Day and another officer at his Fourth Street cottage—approached the corpse, lowered his double-barreled shotgun to Charles's chest and exclaimed, "Now who says I am a coward!" To prove his bravery, Trenchard emptied both barrels into Charles's already desiccated chest.[156]

THE REACTION TO CHARLES'S death was predictable. While some whites emitted a modicum of respect, most believed the "fiend" got off easy. Henry Hearsey from the *States* wrote of Charles, "Never before was such a display of desperate courage on the part of one man witnessed. I cannot help feeling for him a sort of admiration, prompted by his wild and ferocious courage."[157] Later, a city official would express much of the establishment's view of Charles: "The nigger's alright in his place [but] when he tries to get out of it, hit him on the head, and next time he'll come in with his hat off."[158]

The black community, on the other hand, had a different view of Charles. Ida B. Wells-Barnett, a black journalist and contemporary of Charles, sought to uncover the true identity of the man after his death. That proved to be difficult. Charles had been a deep thinker who'd enjoyed sharing his thoughts with others. But otherwise, he had kept a low profile. Also, in the days before and after his death, Charles had become one of the most vilified men in the country. Few of his acquaintances (all of whom were black) wanted to risk retaliation by defending his name or just hinting that he might have acted in self-defense.

However, one man—anonymous, naturally—wrote a letter to Wells-Barnett in which he described his six-year relationship with Charles. The writer claimed that Charles had never been in trouble while in New Orleans before his shootouts with police. Charles had been a quiet and peaceful man. The author of the letter included a copy of one of the documents Charles had been circulating before his death. "Until our preachers preach this document we will always be slaves," Charles had written. "If you can help circulate this 'crazy' doctrine I would be glad to have you do so, for I shall never rest until I get to that heaven on earth; that is, the west coast of Africa, in Liberia."[159]

Ida B. Wells-Barnett summed up what Charles meant to black people all over the nation: "The white people of this country may charge that he was a desperado, but to the people of his own race Robert Charles will always be regarded as the hero of New Orleans."[160]

Hero or villain, cop killer or cop victim, Robert Charles demonstrated that the New Orleans of 1900 would imitate its fellow southern cities in terms of race relations. Despite the city's diversity and history of relative tolerance, New Orleans at the dawn of the twentieth century promised to be as divided, cruel and oppressive as Jim Crow decided.

Robert Charles never made it to Liberia. He never even made it to his own tomb intact.

From Deepest Tartarus

The Axeman and the Birth of Jazz

1905

The little man with a big temper was standing at the bar listening to the music. He nodded and swayed with the new beat that was making deep inroads into the New Orleans music scene. Next to him stood a fifteen-year-old with an even keener ear for the new sound. He, too, was listening appreciatively as the King blared away on his cornet.

Men were shouting over the music to one another: "That boy could make women jump out the window!" "He has a moan in his cornet that goes all through you!" "I never heard anything like that before!" "That boy plays hot!" "No, he play down-low!"

> *I thought I heard Buddy Bolden say,*
> *Funky butt, funky butt, take it away…*
> *You're nasty, you're dirty, take it away…*
> *I thought I heard Buddy Bolden shout,*
> *Open up that window and let the bad air out.*

King Bolden whipped the crowd into a frenzy. He "mosey walked" up and down the stage in his tight blue pants. One of his suspenders hung over his shoulder, and the patrons had a good view of his red flannel undershirt. Most in the crowd wanted to be Buddy. They wanted his money and his fame, but mostly they wanted his women. Who cared if he had so many that he often had to run away from them?

The two patrons at the bar were lost in the brilliance of the King when a mountain of a man stepped forward for a drink. In the process, he stepped on the little man's foot. The two began to shout over the rest of Bolden's shouting fans. The adolescent was stuck between the two belligerents. Suddenly, the little man pulled out a pistol and fired right by the teenager's head and into his large antagonist. The latter crumpled to the floor, dead. Later, the teenager would recall, "This big guy lay there on the floor, dead, and, my goodness, Buddy Bolden—he was up on the balcony with the band—started blazing away with his trumpet, trying to keep the crowd together. Many of us realized it was a killing and we started breaking out windows and through doors and just run over the police they had there."

Shortly after, Bolden himself was arrested. His music evidently appealed to the "rough Negro element" of society. It wasn't "traditional" enough for his white counterparts. It wasn't "sweet" enough for his Creole brethren. No, this new sound was too harsh, too undisciplined, too subversive.

All of these *not enough*s and *too*s were lost on the fifteen-year-old who stood at the bar that night. The boy, who would become known as "Jelly Roll" Morton, would grow up to spread Buddy Bolden's style more than perhaps any other jazz musician.[161]

August 13, 1910

He sat on a doorstep on the corner of Lesseps and Dauphine (the present-day site of Vaughan's Lounge), calmly smoking a cigarette and admiring the caged bird he had just acquired. It was a beautiful mockingbird and had been someone else's pet. They wouldn't be needing it now. The man contentedly exhaled a puff of smoke and opened the birdcage. Out flew the bird. He put his shoes back on and continued on his way.

He left the birdcage behind him. He had already dumped the bloodied meat cleaver a block away in the yard of a woman who was frantically screaming for help while her bloodied husband lay moaning at the foot of his bed.[162]

"RESPECTABLE" NEW ORLEANIANS BELIEVED that vice was a three-headed beast, composed of blacks, Italians and jazz. Historian Gary Krist notes, "For the city's privileged white elite, jazz and vice were of a piece, along with blackness generally and, for that matter, Italianness, too. All were forms of contamination—blots on the city's escutcheon that found expression in crime, depravity, drunkenness, lewdness, corruption, and disease."[163]

In reality, New Orleans's crime problem had more to do with poor municipal leadership, a sinking economy and the decision to create Storyville.

Hustling, gambling and fighting had permeated all parts of the Crescent City. It seemed as if New Orleans was a natural breeding ground for the down-and-out. It was an exotic, beautiful land, blessed with a large harbor at the tail end of one of the world's mightiest rivers. It naturally attracted business, investors and wealthy bon vivants. It also attracted gators, snakes and parasites—animal and human.

All efforts to contain and eliminate vice had failed and failed miserably. The city's leadership decided to try a different tactic: segregate vice as the city had already segregated blacks. Alderman Sidney Story developed the idea for a restricted district of eighteen blocks in which all forms of vice would be tolerated. The city council and the mayor approved the plan, and Storyville (in honor—and much to the chagrin—of Alderman Story) became a reality on January 1, 1898. All gamblers, prostitutes and scoundrels were forced to move their business inside the eighteen-block radius or be shut down. Soon after, a Black Storyville emerged nearby so as to keep blacks (those who were neither musicians nor desirable sex workers) away from the white vice district. They would have their own place to debauch themselves.[164]

1910

The King was dead. Well, not actually dead, but he might as well have been. Buddy Bolden was arrested and declared legally insane in 1907. He would spend the last twenty-four years of his life at the insane asylum in Jackson, Louisiana. His Highness's departure had left quite a vacuum.

The new music needed a new King. One King. Freddie Keppard assumed the mantle, and it fit him well. He intended to wear it a long time. Many other musicians wanted the crown, but only one man—who had "discovered" music late in life and was eight years older than Keppard—had the talent, the presence and the cojones to play the role of usurper.

One evening while at Aberdeen's in Storyville, the "second best Jass man in New Orleans" sat listening to the patrons praising King Freddie Keppard. The adoration went on and on. Unable to take it anymore, the envious, confident man marched toward the stage. He told the piano man the key he wanted, picked up his cornet and began to play. "The notes tore out clear as a bell, crisp and clean. He played as he never had before, filling the little dance hall with low, throbbing blues." He strutted through the bar and out onto the sidewalk, playing all the while. Finally, he stopped. He glared across the street at Frank Lala's where Keppard played. Like Babe Ruth famously calling his homerun, the challenger pointed his cornet at his target and began to play again. "A few hot blasts brought crowds out of both joints; they saw [the upstart] on the sidewalk, playing as if he would blow down every house on the street. Soon every rathole and crib down the line was deserted by its patrons…bewitched by his cornet." He continued blowing until his lungs nearly burst. And still he played, now leading the crowd into Aberdeen's, where he again mounted the stage. He stopped playing long enough to shout, "There! That'll show them!"

Henceforward, the crowds would greet him as King Joe Oliver.[165]

September 20, 1910

Joseph and Concetta Rissetto had been married for seventeen years. They were childless, but they had each other. And they had their grocery. After five years of building a clientele in the black section of Tonti Street, the two expanded their store and added a poolroom, barroom and large cottage in which they kept each other company.

September 19, 1910, had been a usual Monday for the successful couple, and in the evening, they fell asleep together. Several hours later, a man stood above Concetta with a knife and a meat axe. He used the former to delicately slice through the mosquito netting surrounding their bed. The latter came swiftly and violently down upon her sleeping head. It crushed her right cheekbone. When Concetta instinctively rolled over, he sliced the left side of her face and her neck. Then he calmly walked around the bed to where a deep-sleeping Joseph was unaware of the attack. The axe struck Joseph twice, tearing through the cartilage in his nose.

A pained, stunned and blood-blinded Joseph rolled out of bed, hit the floor with a thud and crawled to retrieve the pistol he kept on a dresser. He made his way to the porch and fired two shots into the air.

A Man Murders His Mother with an Axe, by Jan Luyken. *From Rijksmuseum.*

Moments later, the first of many neighbors arrived at the Rissetto house. Joseph was sitting by the bed holding his head and begging someone to help his wife. Concetta lay in bed—her body blood-soaked and her face like a sliced watermelon. She was moaning for help, but the Rissettos lived in the black part of town, on the outskirts of New Orleans, so the roads were poor and public services meager. Help would not arrive quickly.

Terrified neighbors called an ambulance and then carried the dying couple four blocks, past potholes and ditches, to a spot where the ambulance waited to take the couple to Charity Hospital.

Against all odds, both Joseph and Concetta survived. But neither could provide any clues to investigators. Joseph lived for only another two years, badly scarred and blind in one eye. His wife would live another three decades, also scarred and without the husband she had loved for nineteen years.

The axeman had taken nothing from the house. His only intent had been to murder and splatter copious amounts of blood across the grocers' home. His mission accomplished, he left to prowl the streets of New Orleans, looking for his next victim.[166]

CHIEF OF DETECTIVES JAMES Reynolds sat in his office smiling and joking and smoking with his men. He enjoyed these moments. And his men appreciated him. Reynolds was a popular detective. He was hardworking and talented but also laid-back and easy-going. Despite his joshing around, he was concerned. Two similarly gruesome assaults in one month. And both remained unsolved. Reynolds had a suspect, a known dope addict, but the second attack had occurred while the suspect was behind bars. The Crutti and Rissetto assaults mystified him. They were not simple robberies. Neither couple appeared to have enemies capable of such violence.

Even as he smoked and laughed, Reynolds feared he had a deranged fiend on his hands. He worried that because the criminal had attempted to kill without motive, he likely would do so again.

The chief then turned his thoughts to another recurring problem: the Black Hand, or Mafia, as some called the clandestine organization that had sent threats via letter and then bombed uncooperative businesses when they didn't pay the demanded extortion. Perhaps the two—the bombings and the axe attacks—were intimately related. But, then again, perhaps not.[167]

STORYVILLE AND ITS CONCOMITANT vice still flourished, but at least the Axeman had moved on. Or so everyone hoped. At any rate, there had not been an attack in more than half a decade.

Reformers still had their hands full taking on the restricted district. Year after year, they sought to close down the Sodom of the South—to turn New Orleans into a veritable city upon a hill. Year after year, they failed. Hustling, gambling and drinking continued unabated. And then there was the jazz.

1916

The shy, likable teenager had another mouth to feed. He had graciously agreed to raise his third cousin's illegitimate child when she died in childbirth. And then there was his mother and sister. Four mouths to feed now. His music career had stagnated, and his coal cart delivery job could buy only so much food. And there was the rent. And the clothes. And his mule, Lucy.

Louis Armstrong in 1953. *From Library of Congress.*

Needing money, the adolescent turned to hustling. He found himself a girl, "short and nappy-haired and she had buck teeth." But the demand for sex was insatiable in New Orleans, and she made her young pimp enough to support his family.

Yes, his fortunes had seemed to turn. And then they turned again. His milk train, Nootsy, was turning tricks for the men her naïve and affable pimp sent her way, but she had set her sights on one man in particular: her employer. One evening she tried her hardest to get him into bed with her. He demurred, claiming he had never spent a night away from his mother and mule.

"Aw, hell. You are a big boy now. Come in and stay."

When he refused again, Nootsy leapt up and sunk a pocketknife into his shoulder. He ran home and tried to hide the wound from his mother. The tiny house afforded him no such opportunity. Mama Mayann rushed out of the house to confront (or worse) Nootsy. The prostitute was terrified when the enraged mother grabbed her by the throat and shouted, "Don't ever bother my boy again. You are too old for him. He did not want to hurt your feelings, but he don't want no more of you."

Louis Armstrong never pimped again. From then on, music would be his avocation.[168]

August 2, 1917

Terry Mullen had not been paid in weeks. He was hungry. He needed to be paid. He needed to be paid today.

Six-foot-four-inch "Big Terry" walked into police headquarters on Tulane Avenue and South Saratoga Street, intent on getting his money. He had spent the last month on leave because his boss thought he saw signs of mental instability. Now he was desperate.

Terry went straight to Chief James Reynolds's office and begged for his job, and his pay, back. Reynolds insisted that he be medically cleared first.

"When am I going to work?"

"As soon as you are fit."

"Ain't I fit now?"

"Dr. Bayon will have to say when you are fit."

Terry slammed his fist into the chair and screamed, "I'm hungry. I must have money. I tell you, I must have money. I must have money, do you understand?"

Reynolds ordered the agitated giant arrested. But Terry came for money, not time in the tank. He fought back. He broke free of the arresting officer and went straight for his chief. The two wrestled just outside the office. The other cop drew his gun and fired at Terry but missed. Terry drew his own gun and fired. Half a second later, Chief of Police James Reynolds was lying dead on the floor with a bullet in his brain and a hole in his left eye.

Terry shot another officer before trying to make his escape. A pursuing cop shot him in the arm, and Terry meekly surrendered.

He never stood trial. Instead, he was declared insane and sent to the insane asylum in Jackson, Louisiana—where he would be inmates with Buddy Bolden—until his death in 1933.[169]

May 22, 1918

After fifteen years of marriage, and many more building up his grocery business, Joseph Maggio was a contented man. He would have liked to have had children, but his loving wife and financial success made up for this lack.

Joseph had taken charge of the family when his Sicilian father had died. He sailed across the Atlantic to New Orleans, saved his money and then sent for his extended family back in Sicily. He took good care, not only of his beloved wife, Catherine, who worked with him seven days a week in his store, but also of his three brothers and his nieces and nephews. His youngest brother, Andrew, lived in the apartment next door. Both the whites and the blacks in the neighborhood respected Joseph. To the whites, he was "one of the good Italians," hardworking, frugal and patriotic. He bought war bonds and carried a Red Cross pledge card. The blacks called the couple Mr. and Mrs. Joe, and the Maggios served both races from their corner grocery, with its adjoining house at the corner of Magnolia and Upperline.

On Thursday, May 22, 1918, Joseph walked the few steps from his grocery to his bedroom. He had deposited $650 in the bank the day before, and his wife was waiting in the bedroom for him. Joseph and Catherine lay in bed, side by side. Two fortunate Italians who had escaped the violence of Sicily and were living the American dream.

Around four o'clock in the morning, Joseph was jolted awake. Disoriented, stunned and barely conscious, he felt the second blow crash into his skull, fracturing it. Something cold then raced across his face and cheek just before he felt the stinging pain and then the warm blood.

Group of Italians talking on Decatur Street, by Russell Lee, 1938. *From Library of Congress.*

Catherine began to scream and jumped out of bed to protect her husband. She, too, felt the cold, wet slash, the sting and the blood on her face. She twisted away and the razor slashed through her shoulder. She raised her hand to defend herself, and it slashed her hand. The razor slashed her six times before it was placed against her neck. The hand behind it pushed it deep into the right side of her neck and then dragged it across to the left side, severing her jugular vein and carotid artery. Catherine collapsed to the floor, gasping for air. With each gasp, she sucked the blood into her throat and soon drowned in her own blood.

The New Orleans police arrived on the scene early Thursday morning, May 23, 1918. They had been told of the murder by Jacob Maggio, the brother of Joseph. What they saw inside the Maggio house that morning would be forever burned in their minds.

Joseph lay in bed, feet dangling over the edge, covered in blood—some his, some his wife's. The axe blows had evidently incapacitated him before he could even rise. As the detectives and recently arrived ambulance workers watched, Joseph took his final breath and choked as he exhaled it. Catherine was lying on the floor next to the bed with a puddle of blood all around her and her clothes soaked through. There was blood all over the floor, all over the bed, all over the bodies. There was blood splattered seven feet high on the wall.

Only one thing terrified the new police chief and his force more than the ferocious brutality of the attack: the thought that the Axeman had returned.[170]

JUNE 19, 1918

Life had been good to the King. At least as good as life could get for a black man in the Jim Crow South. He had several opportunities to leave New Orleans behind. Many of his fellow jazzmen had left for more lucrative offers in Chicago, New York and California. But not him. No, he preferred New Orleans—that is until one eventful night in 1918 changed his perspective.

The King and Kid Ory were playing at the Winter Garden. Not long after the band began to play, a fight broke out. Shortly after, paddy wagons arrived, and the police began to herd the fighters, patrons and band members into the vehicles and off to prison.

King Joe Oliver would relinquish his crown that night. Fed up with the indignity of being a black man in New Orleans, he took his talents, like so many other Crescent City jazzmen, to Chicago.[171]

JUNE 20, 1918

With Storyville finally closed, the *Times-Picayune* turned its Victorian attention to the new great threat to propriety and virtue: jazz.

An editorial printed on June 20, 1918, read:

> *Why is the jass music, and, therefore, the jass band? As well ask why is the dime novel or the grease-dripping doughnut? All are manifestations of a low streak in man's tastes that has not yet come out in civilization's wash....*
>
> *In the house [of Music] there is, however, another apartment, properly speaking down in the basement, a kind of servant's hall of rhythm. It is there we hear the hum of the Indian dance, the throb of the Oriental tambourines and kettledrums, the clatter of the clogs, the click of Slavic heels, the thumpty-tumpty of the negro banjo, and in fact, the native dances of a world....*
>
> *In the matter of the jass, New Orleans is particularly interested, since it has been widely suggested that this particular form of musical vice had its birth in this city—that it came, in fact, from doubtful surroundings in our slums. We do not recognize the honor of parenthood, but with such a story in circulation, it behooves us to be last to accept the atrocity in public society, and where it has crept in we should make it a point of civic honor to suppress it. Its musical value is nil, and its possibilities of harm are great.*[172]

The paper's sentiment and message were clear: Jazz was a threat to public morality and ought to be eradicated as soon as practicable.

AUGUST 10, 1918

Joseph Romano staggered by the room in which his two screaming nieces had just watched a tall, heavy-yet-nimble man dart away from their door. Uncle Joe, trying to hold his head together, muttered to the girls, "Something has happened. My head hurts. Call for an ambulance."

Shortly after, the ambulance arrived, and Joseph walked into it of his own power. Two hours later, he was dead. The coroner at Charity Hospital told police that he had died of one blow to the head with a very sharp object that "cut clean to the brain."

Back at his grocery/house at 2336 Gravier Street, next to his blood-soaked bed lay a blood-darkened axe.[173]

March 9, 1919

Charlie and Rosie Cortimiglia wrapped up their daily business in the grocery and then began to prepare for bed. Rosie gave two-year-old Mary one final diaper change and feeding, and then tucked their pride and joy into bed between them. Little Mary was soon fast asleep. Her hardworking parents weren't far behind.

Hours later, an axe-wielding man stood above the peacefully sleeping family. He raised his weapon of choice and brought it down on Charlie's skull. The blade went through the scalp and skull and into the brain. He gave Charlie another quick blow to the head, then rapidly turned his attention to Rosie and smashed in the left side of her head, causing the skull to press into her brain. He continued hacking at her, striking her head and ear several more times. Finally, he turned his fiendish attention to Mary. Her little skull proved the weakest of all.

When neighbors arrived the following morning, they beheld the axeman's most gruesome work yet. Charlie and Rosie were covered in blood on either side of the bed. Mary was still between them. There was blood everywhere—on the bed, the mosquito netting, the wall, the curtains and the floor. A painting of Mary, the mother of God, hung on the wall. She was staring at the dying mother and her dead child.[174]

In ten days, Italians all over New Orleans would be celebrating the feast day of the Virgin Mother's husband, Joseph, the patron saint of a happy death. Charlie Cotimiglia would spend the holiday in Charity Hospital, his swollen brain oozing through his fractured skull. Rosie, at first pronounced beyond help, rallied and dozed in and out of consciousness. Mary Cortimiglia spent St. Joseph's feast day underground, in her tiny, white coffin.[175]

Four days after the attack on the Corimiglias, a chilling letter was printed in the local newspaper:

Hell March 13, 1919
Esteemed Mortal of New Orleans: The Axeman

They have never caught me and they never will. They have never seen me, for I am invisible, even as the ether that surrounds your earth. I am not a human being, but a spirit and a demon from the hottest hell. I am what you Orleanians and your foolish police call the Axeman.

When I see fit, I shall come and claim other victims. I alone know whom they shall be. I shall leave no clue except my bloody axe, besmeared with blood and brains of he whom I have sent below to keep me company.

If you wish you may tell the police to be careful not to rile me. Of course, I am a reasonable spirit. I take no offense at the way they have conducted their investigations in the past. In fact, they have been so utterly stupid as to not only amuse me, but His Satanic Majesty, Francis Josef, etc. But tell them to beware. Let them not try to discover what I am, for it were better that they were never born than to incur the wrath of the Axeman. I don't think there is any need of such a warning, for I feel sure the police will always dodge me, as they have in the past. They are wise and know how to keep away from all harm.

Undoubtedly, you Orleanians think of me as a most horrible murderer, which I am, but I could be much worse if I wanted to. If I wished, I could pay a visit to your city every night. At will I could slay thousands

Canal Street from the Clay Monument, by William Henry Jackson. *From Library of Congress.*

*of your best citizens (and the worst), for I am in close relationship with
the Angel of Death.*

*Now, to be exact, at 12:15 (earthly time) on next Tuesday night, I am
going to pass over New Orleans. In my infinite mercy, I am going to make
a little proposition to you people. Here it is:*

*I am very fond of jazz music, and I swear by all the devils in the nether
regions that every person shall be spared in whose home a jazz band is in
full swing at the time I have just mentioned. If everyone has a jazz band
going, well, then, so much the better for you people. One thing is certain
and that is that some of your people who do not jazz it out on that specific
Tuesday night (if there be any) will get the axe.*

*Well, as I am cold and crave the warmth of my native Tartarus, and it
is about time I leave your earthly home, I will cease my discourse. Hoping
that thou wilt publish this, that it may go well with thee, I have been, am
and will be the worst spirit that ever existed either in fact or realm of fancy.*
—*The Axeman*[176]

Saturdays, 1918–1919

The Brick House, Gretna

He was blowing hard that night. He blew hard every night, but tonight was
different. There was a young gal looking at him with the stuff in her eyes. He
kept playing and began to return that righteous look.

He knew she was a hustler, but she clearly had "the mash" on him. During
the break, he took her upstairs. She stated her price, and he said he'd see her
after the show. She was, after all, "a good-looking Creole gal."

When work concluded at five o'clock in the morning, the two rendezvoused
upstairs and spent the next ten hours together. They would meet numerous
times over the next several months. Then one day, the musician realized that
he had fallen in love with a hustler, Daisy.

After not seeing each other for a couple of weeks, Daisy invited him to her
side of the river, to her house in Gretna. He put on his best (only) suit and set
out for his woman's house.

She greeted him at the door and the two began the preliminaries of
lovemaking with her seated on his lap. All of a sudden, someone began
pounding on the door.

It was Daisy's husband.

He barreled through the door and into the room. Daisy took off running with her lawful man right behind. It took a couple of steps and one punch for him to knock Daisy out cold. The startled paramour took off running and didn't stop until he was safely on the ferry going back to New Orleans.

Louis Armstrong vowed to never mess with another's man's wife ever again.[177]

October 27, 1919

The circus was in town. This was fantastic news for Mike Pepitone and his wife, Esther. The couple ran a grocery on the corner of Ulloa and Scott in New Orleans's Mid-City, just one block away from the action. Consequently, they spent all day Saturday and Sunday selling soft drinks to scores of eager children and their parents. It had been a good but exhausting day. Mike went to bed and immediately fell asleep. Esther joined him not long after, around midnight, and she, too, drifted off into a deep sleep.

Around one o'clock in the morning, Esther heard a voice calling her in her sleep. The voice grew louder and louder, closer and closer. Finally, she woke up to hear Mike moaning next to her. She screamed, sat up and shook her husband. "Mike! Mike, what happened?" He only moaned in return. Then she saw what had been his face. It was now just a mush of blood, bone and brain.

Two hours later, Mike Pepitone died at Charity Hospital. His skull had been fractured in several places on both sides. The blood had speckled the wall up to ten feet above the bed, and a fourteen-inch iron bar lay bloodied on the floor.

The police who arrived on the scene knew that they had either another Italian Black Hand vendetta or an axeman attack on their hands.[178]

ONE HUNDRED YEARS AFTER the last Axeman attack, one hundred years after the closing of Storyville and one hundred years after many of the most talented of the jazzmen fled the segregated Crescent City, New Orleans still has a soft spot for vice, can still be a dangerous place to live and is still the world's most inspiring city for up-and-coming jazzmen.

The "legalized" vice of Storyville has moved to the more respectable Bourbon Street and Central Business District, where Harrah's Casino and a plethora of strip clubs and jazz joints operate with near impunity. Of course, the vice squad makes sporadic crackdowns—sex workers are sometimes slapped on the wrist, a drug dealer is a little too obvious plying his trade with tourists and occasionally a few visitors stand blocking the doorway of a club, transfixed, while a woman lifts her shirt and bra in exchange for a set of plastic beads. They are asked to move so other inebriated patrons can enter the bar and get a few Abita cups to go.

Yes, vice and New Orleans go together like red beans and rice. All people are a mixture of sin and godliness. It's just that New Orleans is a good deal more open and tolerant in regard to the former.

Reader, do you know who the Axeman was? No? Well, no one does. Do you know the names Lulu White, Josie Arlington or Willie Piazza—famous Storyville madams? If you do, then either you are a veritable history aficionado, or your grandfather told you some interesting stories from his youth. Have you ever listened to jazz or heard the voice of Louis Armstrong? Of course, you have. And that's the point. The murderers, thugs and destroyers played an important role in the history of New Orleans. Now, they are gone and forgotten. It is the artists, musicians and creators who are destined to represent New Orleans as long as there is a New Orleans.

It is the jazzmen, not the pimps, gamblers and killers (although sometimes, the line between the two is blurred), who have made *New Orleans* a universal byword and one of the world's top tourist destinations. It is the artists, not the criminals, who guarantee that New Orleans will endure.

8

DYNAMITE BANDITS

Terrorist Tactics in the Carmen's Strike of 1929

As North Claiborne No. 816 rolled past the tombs of Saint Louis No. 2 cemetery, Cinderella Denton sat midway down the car. There were ten other passengers in the car at the time, but Denton was really the only passenger—the other ten were crewmen. Cars had required more crewmen—sometimes armed with sawed-off shotguns—since the strike had begun seven weeks before.[179]

Denton sat by herself. And then BOOM, a section of the car's floor disappeared in front of her. She was on the floor, or what was left of it. She stood up, wobbly, and made her way to the back. She stepped out, then blacked out and hit the tracks. She didn't wake again until she was in a hospital bed.

Denton's streetcar had run over a dynamite charge placed there moments before by an unscrupulous supporter of an ongoing strike by employees of New Orleans Public Service Incorporated (NOPSI), which owned and operated New Orleans's streetcars. The streetcar had run over an improvised explosive device.

The dynamite ripped a hole in the wooden floor of the car and sent an eighteen-inch length of steel rail up through the ceiling, leaving a large hole in its wake. If the rail had hit Denton, she'd have been killed. The airborne rail continued sailing through the air, narrowly missing another woman walking along the sidewalk. The iron missile cracked into the brick wall of the cemetery where the old pirate Dominique You lay, steps in front of the woman.

St. Charles Street circa 1900—Detroit Publishing Company. *From the Beinecke Library at Yale University.*

The other ten men who'd been inside the car stumbled out, temporarily "stunned," as they were likely suffering from the invisible wounds of a close-range blast, including concussion, hearing loss and organ damage from the powerful "stress wave" emanated. Denton's symptoms, too, seem consistent with the invisible shock suffered by soldiers in proximity to IED blasts—rapid heartbeat, loss of muscle tone resulting in a "rag-doll appearance," and drastically lowered blood pressure. Denton was unresponsive for a time after the blast, suggesting that she may have been suffering from a kind of deep shock that affects a minority of blast victims.[180]

Almost five miles away, on the shore of Lake Pontchartrain, pedestrians stopped, wondering about the strange boom they'd heard coming from the direction of the French Quarter. One woman near the blast fell over in her automobile, unconscious.

The pedestrians in the vicinity of the blast rushed toward the streetcar, quickly forming a crowd. Police arrived and, feeling the need to disperse the crowd that had grown to encompass four city blocks, began detonating tear gas bombs. A work crew arrived shortly after and went about fixing the destroyed section of rail, which was under heavy guard.

The bombing of North Claiborne No. 816 was not the first time the carmen's strike had turned violent, but it marked a dangerous new milestone in how far strikers would go to scare people away from riding the city's streetcars. Unfortunately for the city, the bombing of streetcars would not stop for months. Several dozen streetcar bombings would rock the city, terrorizing commuters and bystanders.

And when all was said and done, the drastic tactics resorted to by the city's streetcar strikers would prove to be ineffective. The strike would go down in American history not only as one of the most violent but also as one of the most disastrous.

THE CITY STREET AT the turn of the twentieth century began to grow increasingly important as a vital artery. The street performed its traditional functions of conveying people to work or to shop, but it began to take on new responsibilities as well. Streets allowed city services, such as the fire and police departments, to function. Streets provided the latticework necessary for installing and supplying public utilities. And as new technologies such as the electric streetcar were coming into existence, streets provided ready-made maps of where streetcar lines should go.

New Orleans took to the streetcar early, building one of the first streetcar lines in the United States in 1835 (New York City was the first city to build a street railway in 1831). New Orleans's first lines ran from the city to the suburb of Carrollton, and cars were powered by either steam engine or horse or mule.[181]

The streetcar was looked on as such a huge improvement over horses that it became, in only a few years, an indispensable part of city life that shaped the city residents' routines and expectations.

New Orleans continued to refine and expand its streetcar network throughout the 1800s (even experimenting with a horse-drawn canal barge). New Orleans's street railway networks began electrification in 1893, with full modernization coming by 1902. From 1922 to 1926, New Orleans's streetcar networks, which until then had been operated by nine separate companies, were absorbed into New Orleans Public Service Incorporated. By 1926, the peak of ridership in New Orleans, the city boasted twenty-six streetcar lines. An astonishing 148 million passengers rode New Orleans's streetcars that year.[182]

The populace of New Orleans had grown reliant on the city's streetcars, and streetcar workers knew it. They sensed, as scholar Delos F. Wilcox pondered in 1904, that "in proportion to the usefulness of a thing is its power over us....A tie-up of the lines means a very serious paralysis of city life." The streetcar's intensive infrastructure requirements (fixed tracks, invariable routes, electric power supply, storage barns) had also made it vulnerable to those seeking to use its smooth functioning as a bargaining chip. When streetcar workers decided a strike was in order, control over the streetcar network was relatively easily achievable, and "the control of the streets," Wilcox wrote, "means the control of the cities."[183]

Streetcar workers across the country realized the power they held over cities, and strikes became more frequent and nastier by the first decades of the century. Employers began taking drastic measures to get even with striking laborers.[184] Those drastic measures took the form of imported scabs who were either entrepreneurial soldiers-of-fortune or the most detestable criminal dregs of society, depending on who you asked.[185] The strikebreakers were certainly risk-tolerant, and strikebreakers and strikers would engage in "warfare" in city streets, drawing comparisons to the Civil War battles of a generation before.[186] Of course, strikers did their part to push protests toward violence.

And violence is exactly the direction in which the carmen's strike of 1929 headed, quickly and forcefully. The carmen's union called the strike on the night of July 1, 1929. At issue was New Orleans Public Service's refusal to agree to two of the workers' demands. Workers wanted a "closed shop" provision, which would prevent the company from hiring nonunion workers. They also wanted to make it harder for the company to fire employees. Twelve hundred NOPSI workers stopped working, and 351 streetcars were parked in their barns, intended by the strikers to stay there until an agreement was reached.[187]

For three days, streetcars sat in their barns, and striking carmen waited to see whether NOPSI would agree to their demands. NOPSI, in return, waited for the striking carmen to relent and return to work. Of course, NOPSI refused to let its streetcars sit in the barns indefinitely—it had begun planning to break the strike since before it was even called. NOPSI gave the striking workers until 6:00 p.m. on July 4 to relent. If they didn't, the corporation would restart streetcar service using an army of 850 imported strikebreakers from other parts of the country.[188]

JULY 4

Six o'clock came and went with no agreement made between New Orleans Public Service Incorporated and its striking workers. NOPSI chose Canal Street as its preferred battleground to open its war against the strikers. Four hundred strikebreakers were marched to the Canal Street barn just minutes after the 6:00 p.m. deadline passed. NOPSI would begin sending the strikebreakers, along with two hundred employees who had refused to go on strike, to different parts of the city to resume streetcar service. One hundred New Orleans police officers escorted the strikebreakers. An army of six hundred strikers was waiting for the men at the Canal Street barn.[189]

As the two groups converged, with the strikebreakers marching in lines, strikers opened hostilities with volleys of "Irish confetti," thrown bricks and stones. A reporter's notes from the evening describe what seems more like a pitched battle than a riot: "In a few moments, as the rain of missiles became thicker and thicker, the strike breakers broke from the orderly ranks

Canal Street empty of streetcars but full of automobiles early in the 1929 strike. *From collection of H. George Friedman Jr.*

into which they had formed after detraining at St. Louis and North White Streets and sought shelter, abandoning their luggage in their mad flight. The strikers followed the fleeing men, many of whom were already bloody, and numerous hand-to-hand encounters developed."[190]

Fifteen minutes of fisticuffs followed, then "guns began to bark promiscuously," a report described, "And the lust for blood was on." Police fired dozens of shots into the air, but one shot hit a man instead—fifty-six-year-old Joseph Morlinerio, an eleven-year employee of NOPSI who was fighting on the side of the strikers (an investigation into the shooting found that the fatal shot was fired by an "unknown person"). After Morlinerio fell to the pavement, blood "gurgling from his throat," the riot abruptly stopped. Police commandeered a car and took Molinerio to the hospital. The Canal Street riot had cooled down, but another riot erupted at the Arabella station.[191]

One hundred fifty of the strikebreakers who had sought shelter in the Canal Streetcar barn, where medical personnel had established a makeshift hospital, were bused to other parts of the city later that night. Strikers were savvy to the company's plans and met the strikebreakers at stoplights, pelting the buses with more stones and bricks. The carmen's strike had officially turned violent, and NOSPI had not actually tried to begin running any streetcars yet. The first car would run the following day, with disastrous results.

In the three days before officially trying to restart streetcar service, NOPSI inspectors had received clues that strikers might resort to terroristic tactics to prevent streetcars from running. Several of the company's switch boxes, which controlled the tracks that streetcars traveled along, were found to have been filled with cement, rendering them useless. In addition, the inspectors feared that dynamite had been embedded in the concrete as booby traps placed to detonate upon the strike of a pickaxe. The boxes were cut whole from the rails and dumped into the Mississippi River.[192]

The following day, July 5, proved that the riots of the previous evening had been only a taste of the violence that would come. At seven o'clock that morning, NOPSI made good on its promise to resume streetcar service using strikebreakers and armed guards. The move was purely symbolic—no sane New Orleans resident would dare ride the streetcar that day.

The Canal Street barn was again the focal point of the violence. The first streetcar left the barn with four armed policemen as its passengers. It was immediately pelted with stones and bricks. The car made its way along its route through the business district, pelted all the way by strikers on foot and in cars.

Marshals guarding a battered streetcar. *From Internet Archive.*

In the business district, an elderly black man who was somehow unaware that the strike was still in effect hailed the streetcar, and it stopped. The man paid ten cents for his fare, and while waiting for his change, was hit in the head with a brick. The man scrambled under a seat and began to pray. He rode all the way back to the barn, then fled in terror. He had been the journey's sole customer.[193]

The streetcar actually made one complete loop, albeit with its windows broken out, and tried going out for a second one. Doubling down on their resistance, strikers tried even harder to punish the car and its occupants. They succeeded, actually stopping the car with the massive amount of debris thrown. The police guards fired into the crowd of rioters, dropping two men before reversing course. Women in the crowd begged the policemen not to shoot, and the men with guns in the crowd returned fire. Many unarmed men left, vowing to return with their own guns.[194]

The NOPSI tried once more to run the Canal Street car later that day. This time, the car was not only stopped by a crowd that had swelled to twenty thousand, but the crew also had to be rescued and evacuated. The empty car, sitting at the foot of Canal Street, was doused with gasoline and burned. When firemen arrived to put out the fire, rioters cut their hoses.

Rioters in other parts of the city set about sabotaging rail, tearing it up in some places, covering it with piles of dirt in others and pouring molten lead over it in others. Another car and a NOPSI shed were burned. One streetcar crew made a loop of the St. Charles line, but its car "returned to the barn with every window shattered," a report read, "And every man within bearing bruises and cuts caused by endless barrages of bricks."[195]

Some policemen and NOPSI repairmen, upon seeing the carnage, simply quit. Other men showed courage, such as policeman Gaston Lopes who had his kneecap shattered by a brick while riding on a streetcar near Canal Street. He begged to be allowed to stay on duty but was sent home.[196]

When the day's rioting ended, two men had been killed, several hundred people had been injured and an estimated $50,000 worth property had been destroyed (about $750,000 today).[197] NOPSI's attempt at breaking the strike had been met by an outpouring of ferocious violence. The coming weeks would show that strikers and their sympathizers would not shy from using the most devious tactics to force the company's hand.

"THEIR SUPPLY HAD RUN out and they needed more to use on streetcars to scare people from riding the cars."

Albert Bendix was spilling the beans for federal investigators. He had been caught smuggling dynamite into the carmen's union headquarters at St. Claude and Bartholomew Streets. He told the investigators how they'd been getting the dynamite, where they'd been storing it and how they'd been using it.

Terror was the explicit purpose of planting the dynamite bombs, Bendix said. He'd seen it being moved to the headquarters many times, always at night. St. Claude Street, which ran in front of the union headquarters, served as a popular illicit drive-through for strikers looking to deposit or withdraw bomb-making supplies. Bendix told investigators that he'd personally witnessed many of the illicit transactions that took place on St. Claude Street in front of the union headquarters: "On many occasions men would drive up in front of the place in automobiles and the man driving would call one of the picket men and ask what they had."[198]

Strikers had turned to dynamite as a means of intimidation since the earliest days of the strike. On July 5, the carnage-filled day that New Orleans Public Service Incorporated had tried to restart streetcar service, strikers had thrown sticks of dynamite into the Poland Street barn.[199]

Strikers began using dynamite to fashion IEDs in August, with the August 21 bombing of North Claiborne No. 816 the first to make national news. As Bendix had told investigators days before, the dynamite used in the blasts had been stolen.[200] What the incident also confirmed was that even with federal authorities busting up the union headquarters–centered dynamite smuggling ring, the bombings would not stop. Ridership on New Orleans's streetcars was down 90 percent, from about 380,000 passengers daily to 38,000.[201]

For a few weeks, with the prospect of a settlement between NOPSI and the union looking good, violence died down. Then in September, strikers rejected a settlement deal (NOPSI refused to guarantee they'd hire back the workers who'd gone on strike), and the violence and bombings started again.

On September 11, the same day strikers rejected the settlement deal, a dynamite bomb blew a car on Washington Avenue right off its tracks. The three passengers and the crew were unhurt.[202] A couple of days later, a car full of strikers pulled up alongside a streetcar traveling along the Esplanade line and threw a bundle of five sticks of dynamite into the car. Showing remarkable accuracy, the bomb-thrower hit the streetcar's conductor in the leg with the package. Luckily for him, it did not explode. The strikers were showing that they were not just content to destroy NOPSI property but also wanted to spill blood.[203]

Police, seeking desperate measures to answer the bombings, were given orders to arm themselves with shotguns and shoot to kill.[204] "Use your weapons, your shotguns and pistols if you come across these dynamiters," one captain told his officers. "This bombing of street cars must cease."[205] Newspapers branded the bomb-planting strikers as "dynamite bandits."[206]

By October, a dozen street cars had been bombed, and other attempts at blowing up cars had been foiled.[207] The bombings continued through the fall and winter, occurring with more frequency. By January, the number of cars bombed had climbed to sixty-four.[208]

As the strikers' bombing campaign intensified, something else was happening—the strikers were losing their will to hold out. Through the months of July, August and September, strikers had stood together, with less than 1 percent returning to NOPSI to resume working. But with fall setting in and workers and their families feeling the pressure of lost wages (and attendant hunger), workers began returning to the company by the hundreds. By November 1, more than four hundred of the strikers, a third of the workers who had originally gone on strike, had returned to NOPSI.

Despite the ferocious tactics that strikers had used to try to force NOSPI's hand, the strike was losing its potency. NOPSI was winning.

⌐─ ··· ─⌐

Supply. The union could cut the supply of streetcars to passengers and of crewmen to run those streetcars.

The success or failure of the 1929 carmen's strike came down to a matter of supply and demand. Strikers wanted to cut the supply of streetcars to New Orleans's citizens and drive up demand and public outcry, leading to an eventual capitulation by New Orleans Public Service Incorporated. NOPSI wanted to keep the streetcars running and customers happy. Preventing the streetcars from running, by strike, bombing or other means, was the strikers' means of limiting supply. Bringing in strikebreakers and armed marshals to force the resumption of streetcar service was NOPSI's means of maintaining supply.

Supply. That was the lever both sides were fighting over.

Demand. That was not something as easily manipulatable by the carmen's union and NOPSI. If customers were given the choice of a different cheap and convenient means of transportation, demand for streetcar service might wane, thereby destroying the union's bargaining token and diminishing NOPSI's ridership. That would be bad for both sides of the dispute, but which side would suffer more? As it turned out, the union would.

New transportation sprouted up as the carmen's strike heated up: the taxicab or "jitney," as it was called then.

Fourteen years before the carmen's strike of 1929, the City of New Orleans had passed an ordinance aimed at squashing the burgeoning jitney industry. The city required that every jitney be bonded for $5,000—a measure ostensibly aimed at ensuring public safety. The practical effect of the law was that every jitney operator had to pay $190 (around $5,000 today) to have his or her car bonded. The fee was so high that no jitney driver could pay it, and the ordinance effectively crushed the industry. Although public safety was the purported reason for passing the law, legal scholars of the time noted that the law and laws similar to it in other cities were clearly benefiting the streetcar companies, effectively putting the companies' competition out of business.[209]

The jitney ordinance had killed the industry in New Orleans, but the demand for alternatives to the streetcars tempted many automobile owners in New Orleans to become illicit jitney drivers during the 1929 strike. Thirteen hundred jitneys began running during the strike, carrying passengers throughout New Orleans in defiance of the 1915 ordinance. By comparison, only one hundred jitneys had been operating in the city at the time the ordinance was passed.[210]

The striking carmen were presented with a conundrum: as long as the jitneys were running, citizens would use them instead of NOPSI's streetcars. NOPSI would lose passengers and revenue. On the other hand, as long as citizens had an alternative to the streetcar, there wouldn't be as much public demand for an end to the strike. Citizens would be able to go about their lives without feeling the pressure of the loss of the streetcars.

The strikers decided that hurting NOPSI's bottom line was more important than ratcheting up public discomfort. The strikers decided not only to support the jitney trade but also to demand that the city repeal the ordinance forbidding jitneys from running.

On August 13, around the time that the strikers' streetcar-bombing campaign was starting in earnest, a group of union members presented a petition with fifty thousand signatures to city commissioners meeting at City Hall. The petition called for the revocation of the 1915 ordinance. Acting mayor T. Semmes Walmsley told the group that he and the city commissioners would consider the petition. Incensed that Walmsley did not immediately take action, members of the group "set upon" the mayor and city council. Walmsley and several city council members were punched before police were able to drive the mob out of City Hall.[211]

In the process of quelling the riot, police officers shot four members of the mob. The city hall riot marked yet another violent milestone in the strike. Rather than repealing the jitney ordinance, the city, alarmed at the strikers at city hall, decided to crack down. The day after the riot, Walmsley

Female strike sympathizers throwing brickbats. *From collection of H. George Friedman Jr.*

declared that "anarchy must cease" and that the police would begin strict enforcement of the jitney ordinance. Within a few days, one hundred illegal jitney operators had been arrested.[212] NOPSI, sensing that the tides were turning against the illicit jitney trade, began suing individual jitney drivers.[213]

The decision by strikers to support and encourage the illegal jitney trade was a critical mistake, according to one analyst. J.W. Leigh wrote a multiple-page essay for *Labor Age* magazine examining how and why the strike had turned out to be a "debacle." If strikers had demanded enforcement of the jitney ordinance at the start of the strike, they could have paralyzed the city; traffic to downtown businesses would have been choked off, spurring business owners, along with members of the public and striking workers, to call for a settlement, forcing NOPSI's hand. Instead, jitneys had filled the gap left by the cessation of streetcar traffic, and life had gone on somewhat normally for New Orleans's citizens and businesspeople.

Strikers should have pushed not only for the enforcement of the jitney ordinance, Leigh wrote, but also the obedience to all laws and the prioritization of law and order. Strikers should have stayed at home and waited rather than picketing. Union leaders should have cooperated with police in catching anyone "wreaking vengeance on the property of the Public Service or its employees."[214]

Instead, the strike had gone down in history as one of the most violent ever. And in the end, the extreme tactics employed by the strikers had not amounted to much except some damage to their employer's bottom line and a lot of citizens' pain. In total, 40 million fewer passengers rode New Orleans's streetcars in 1929 than in 1928 and NOPSI lost $2 million in revenue. Five streetcar lines were abolished altogether because of the strike.[215] Several people lost their lives, many hundreds were injured and an entire city was terrorized by a bombing campaign.

The New Orleans carmen's union had forfeited any moral high ground when its members decided to employ the dynamite bomb as a means of instilling terror in their fellow citizens. There is a unique cruelty inherent in the use of such a weapon, according to Shaun Allen, a former Royal Marine and Afghanistan veteran, who now studies the weapons' effects. "IEDs are perhaps amongst the most awful weapons on the battlefield today," Allen writes. "They are inanimate victim-activated explosive devices recognizing neither friend nor foe, making no distinctions between soldiers or civilians."[216]

The carmen's union made the mistake of adopting an ends-justify-the-means strategy, and in the end, its members were left with empty stomachs and blood on their hands.

The Carrollton Streetcar Barn in 2019. *From Josh Foreman.*

MOSQUITOES AND TORPEDOES

New Orleans Goes to War

The sound was loud enough to wake eight-year-old Raymond Downs Jr. "Gee," he thought, "We must be bumping against the dock in New Orleans."

It was 2:00 a.m. on May 19, 1942, and Downs had been sleeping on the top bunk in a little cabin aboard the SS *Heredia*, a freighter hauling bananas and coffee from South America to New Orleans. The Downs family—Raymond and his father, mother and sister—had been living in South America, where Raymond Downs Sr. had been working for New Orleans–based United Fruit Company. The Downs family was heading back to New Orleans because Raymond Downs Sr. wanted to join the marines. The United States had entered World War II six months before, and he wanted to do his part.

The boy heard another sound, clearly an explosion this time, and opened his eyes. His father was staring into his face. He was standing, the boy noticed, in water.

"Put on your life jacket and tie it tight," his dad said. "You stay right here. I'm gonna get your mother and your sister."

Downs's father left the cabin. He followed shortly after. "Staying here," as his father had asked, would not be possible. Downs joined a trail of other passengers and crewmen seeking the top deck of the sinking ship. He had lost track of his father, mother and sister. As the boy searched for a way out, the ship turned at a strange angle. Suddenly, Downs was underwater. He was able to swim to a steel ladder that led to the top deck of the ship—a way out. When he reached the deck, his eyes were blinded by a bright light. He didn't realize the light was coming from another boat—one that had fired a torpedo into the hull of the SS *Heredia*. The light was coming from an enormous ship. A German one. A U-boat.

Eight and a half minutes had passed since Raymond Downs Jr. was awoken by the sound of a torpedo striking his boat, and now the final few inches of the ship's deck were slipping below the water. Downs, too, slipped into the water. Then he spotted someone swimming toward him.

"Dad!"[217]

As RAYMOND DOWNS JR. and his family crossed the Gulf of Mexico in a banana freighter, twenty-two-year-old Denton W. Crocker was working to finish his studies at Northeastern University in Boston. Crocker would graduate with a biology degree the following month. For a while, he'd known exactly what he'd be doing when he graduated: serving his country. Crocker had received a draft notice five months earlier. He would be joining the army, the notice said.[218]

Crocker had grown up in Salem, Massachusetts, a lover of nature who made frequent camping trips to the forests of New Hampshire. Even before the United States entered World War II, Crocker sought to serve, volunteering as an airplane spotter in Salem. Twice a week, he would sit on top of a local high school and log sightings of possible German airplanes. When his draft number came up, he accepted that he'd soon be a soldier but hoped he wouldn't actually have to bear arms for his country. He hoped, instead, to serve in a medical support role.[219]

Crocker left his native New England shortly after graduation and headed for the South. He would undergo basic training at Camp Pickett in Virginia. Crocker's superiors immediately noticed his curiosity and scientific mind and offered him a job as a sanitary technician. In addition to learning basic military skills like marching, patrolling, bed-making and potato-peeling, Crocker took specialized classes in military cleanliness. He had such a good grasp of the material that he was soon asked to become a teacher as well. He studied food- and water-borne diseases, maintaining a clean camp, immunization and, what would turn out to be most important for Crocker, the control of insect-borne diseases.[220]

In 1941, the U.S. Army and U.S. Public Health Service had gotten serious about tackling the problem of mosquitoes and malaria in the South. The

WILLIAM J. COBB

Accounting
142 Vernon Street, Norwood

Activities:
Law and Accounting Club 4, 5, Secretary 3; Swimming Team 1; Track Team 2; Glee Club 1; Class Vice-President 5; Class Executive Council 5; S.A.M.

Cooperative Work:
Wm. Filene's Sons, Boston   Stock Clerk

JOHN M. CONNOR

Electrical Engineering
11 Curtin Street, Mansfield

Activities:
Freshman Honor List; Dean's List 4; Class President 1; A.I.E.E. Executive Committee 2.

Cooperative Work:
Allis-Chalmers Mfg. Co.,   Laboratory
Hyde Park   Assistant

JOSEPH F. COUGHLIN

Chemical Engineering
52 Saunders Road, Norwood

Activities:
Senate-Tau Beta Pi; Freshman Honor List; Dean's List 2, 3, 4.

Cooperative Work:
Bird and Sons, Inc., E. Walpole   Helper on Machine
A. D. Little Co., Cambridge   Assistant Chemist
General Electric Co., W. Lynn   Electroplater

DENTON W. CROCKER

Liberal Arts (Biology)
44 Bellevue Road, Beach Bluff

Cooperative Work:
C. W. Whittier and Bros., Boston   Elevator Operator
Northeastern University, Boston   Laboratory Assistant

48

Denton Crocker's 1942 yearbook page. *From Northeastern University/Internet Archive.*

131

War Department allocated $1.5 million that year for domestic mosquito control. The results of the army's push to fight malaria in the United States were heartening, and the infection rate for soldiers dropped steadily from 1.7 per thousand people annually in 1941 to 0.1 per thousand people annually in 1945. The results showed that the disease—and its insect vector—could be defeated. Crocker seemed to make the army's mission to wipe out malaria his own.[221]

In Virginia, Crocker would frequently hike into the countryside to spot and identify the native fauna, much of which was foreign to him. Crocker found classes boring but delighted in his own independent studies. He purchased field guides on the mosquitoes of the South and was soon surveying Camp Pickett's resident mosquito population. He collected specimens, learned how mosquitoes hatched from larvae and studied the insects under microscopes. His fascination with the mosquito led him so far as to stand in a nearby swamp with his pant legs rolled up, capturing in little tubes the mosquitoes that landed on him.[222]

Crocker's superiors put him in charge of official mosquito collection and identification for the camp. Although Crocker flirted with the idea of attending medical school and becoming an army doctor, it became increasingly clear to the young man that his destiny would lie in an experimental army unit forming in the Deep South. "I guess that a malaria unit is inevitable," he wrote to his parents at home.[223]

The "malaria unit" of which Crocker wrote was actually desperately needed by Allied forces in the Pacific theater. As U.S. and Australian troops began pushing into the islands of the South Pacific, few understood the enormous toll disease would take. Malaria had been present in the American South when the army began trying to tackle the disease, but the South Pacific was positively rife with it.

A parasitic disease carried by the *Anopheles* mosquito, malaria is caused when microscopic parasites called plasmodia travel into the human bloodstream through a mosquito's saliva. The parasites head straight for the liver, where they infect and destroy red blood cells. Malaria causes intense flu-like symptoms—high fever, shaking, weakness—and can cause death (the disease still causes almost half a million deaths per year worldwide), although most cases are not fatal.[224]

Malaria was the most destructive of the tropical diseases troops in the Pacific theater faced. It was so prevalent that the rate of infection was not measured in the number of troops who contracted the disease but in how many times each troop contracted the disease; infection was almost guaranteed. By January 1943, Allied troops in the South Pacific had contracted malaria an average of four times each.[225]

In 1942, military leaders realized malaria was ravaging their troops at Guadalcanal in the Solomon Islands. U.S. and Australian troops were fighting the Japanese for control of the island, but they were fighting even harder against disease. "The greatest single factor reducing troop effectiveness on Guadalcanal was disease, particularly malaria," one historian wrote. "For every man who became a casualty in combat, five fell to malaria." One man would be fighting the disease, another would be lying in a hospital bed sick with malaria and another would be convalescing after getting over the disease.[226]

Japanese troops did not escape the ravages of malaria either. Finding a way to prevent the disease from affecting Allied troops would not only preserve Allied manpower but also break the symmetry of the disease's effects on men. The Japanese would continue to suffer unless they too could take equally effective measures against it. With the battle for Guadalcanal still raging, the Office of the Surgeon General recommended to the commanding general of the U.S. Army Forces, South-West Pacific, that a rigorous plan be implemented to combat the disease overseas. As part of the plan, the army should train special units to study and control the causes of malaria in the places where troops deployed. For every twenty thousand Allied troops in the Pacific, there should be two malaria control units deployed with them— one to study the problem and one to enact solutions. The antimalaria units would travel with soldiers as they hopped across Pacific islands pushing back the Japanese line.[227]

The army went about enacting the plan immediately, experimenting with malaria survey and control field training in Alabama and Florida. But ultimately, the army decided on a different area for its primary unit training center—a bend in the Mississippi River just west of New Orleans. The area, in present-day Harahan, Louisiana, was the site of Camp Plauche, where all the malaria units of World War II were trained. The climate of south Louisiana was suitable for year-round study of the mosquito, and the port of New Orleans was just a few miles away. Soldiers could learn to fight malaria then step onto a ship and sail into the Gulf, bound for the Panama Canal and the Pacific. As a bonus to the soldiers who came from all over the United States, they'd get to carouse in the Big Easy in their downtime.

Crocker, who'd seemed destined for an antimalaria unit for the start, boarded a train and headed for New Orleans.[228]

⌐━━ ·‥ ━━⌐

RAYMOND DOWNS JR. CLIMBED aboard a four-by-four-foot raft of canvas-wrapped wood. Three men, including Downs's father, climbed in too. They were scared that the Germans would rake them with machinegun fire, something the Germans had been known to do,[229] so they paddled hard to get away from the site of the attack. There was still no sign of Downs's mother or sister. Downs's father had been wounded, and his legs were bleeding. They floated in the little life raft for hours, their legs dangling over the side. The sun rose, and the group continued to float some forty miles southwest of New Orleans. Sharks circled the raft. Then dolphins showed up, and the sharks swam away. The day passed, and the sun began to set.

Downs, not understanding the gravity of the situation, asked his dad if they could go in to shore and eat dinner. His dad tried to distract him by pointing out seagulls. One of the birds they spotted was not a bird—it was a navy rescue plane. The plane dropped water, floats and medical supplies and called in a prototype of the civilian "Cajun Navy" that would earn fame rescuing victims of hurricanes decades later—a rescue fleet of shrimpers. A shrimp boat arrived at Downs's location around ten o'clock that night. They had been rescued after floating at sea for the better part of a day.

On their way back to Morgan City, Louisiana, the shrimp boat crew ran across an oil slick and another survivor. They pulled a bedraggled woman aboard and were astonished to find that she was an oil-covered, but otherwise unharmed, Ina Downs—Raymond Downs Jr.'s mother. There was still no sign of Lucille, Downs's sister. Then the radio crackled. Lucille had been rescued by another boat. Against all odds, all four members of the Downs family survived the attack on the SS *Heredia*. Thirty-six other passengers, however, had not.[230]

Adolf Hitler declared war on the United States on December 11, 1941, and decided the next day to launch *Paukenschlag*, or Operation Drumbeat. As part of the operation, German U-boats, which had already been operating in the Atlantic, would attack shipping along North America's coastlines. Hitler designated only six U-boats for operation in North America, sending four times as many to the Mediterranean. The United States would soon learn the destruction a small number of U-boats could sow. By January 1942, U-boats had begun targeting tankers and freighters along the northeast coast.

The Germans found ripe targets for their attacks due to total unpreparedness on the part of the United States. The U-boats did most of their hunting at night when they could avoid detection. The drawback to sinking ships at night, though, was that they were hard to see. For three months after the U-boat attacks began, coastal cities continued shining their lights brightly at night, which silhouetted ships, making targeting them easy.[231]

Fewer than one hundred coast guard vessels were available for antisubmarine patrols along the east coast when the offensive started, and only half a dozen short-range bombers were available for air support. With those meager tools, the United States found itself trying to defend a coastline that stretched from the Canadian border to Florida. "No more perfect set-up for rapid and ruthless destruction could have been offered the Nazi sea lords," the naval historian Samuel Eliot Marison wrote.

In the first two months of the offensive, nearly 120 merchant ships were sunk between the North American coastline and Britain, with the vast majority of them sunk near the North American coastline. Hitler increased the number of U-boats operating on the United States coastlines to forty by midsummer.[232]

As the United States improved its ability to thwart the U-boat attacks along the east coast, the Germans shifted their attention to the Gulf of Mexico, which some experts believed would never be penetrated by German U-boats. If the submarine defenses of the East Coast were inadequate at the start of the offensive, the defenses of the Gulf Coast were downright laughable. To protect the Gulf Coast, the coast guard had at its disposal all of four vessels—three cutters and a converted yacht. Air defenses consisted largely of unarmed observational planes and two antiquated army bombers. The experts who believed a U-boat assault in the Gulf was unlikely were soon proven dead wrong. In May 1942, five months after Operation Drumbeat had begun, half a dozen U-boats cruised into the Gulf, traveling on the surface in darkness and submerging during the day.[233]

The U-boats found plenty of targets in the Gulf, sinking half a dozen merchant ships along the coasts of Mexico and Texas, half a dozen in the open Gulf and a dozen near Cuba. But by far, the Germans targeted ships sailing near the mouth of the Mississippi. The Germans wanted to sink "the greatest possible tonnage of enemy shipping," one historian wrote, "in the shortest possible space of time."[234] Admiral Karl Dönitz, the overall German submarine commander, gambled that the mouth of the Mississippi would be "swarming with ships." He was right.[235]

The water at the mouth of the Mississippi was murky, shallow and moved swiftly. Sailing large submarines there was risky, but the potential payoff was the sinking of many ships and the closure of shipping traffic to and from New Orleans. Dönitz directed U-507 and U-506, two Type IX U-boats, to

A U.S. Coast Guard recruiting poster from the war years. *From Library of Congress.*

head there. The Type IX was the German navy's largest and most capable submarine. It was 252 feet long, carried a crew of forty-eight men and fourteen stealthy, battery-powered torpedoes. The torpedoes could be fired from stern or bow. The Type IX was armed with a 105-millimeter deck gun, which could sink ships as well. It held enough fuel to travel some 12,600 miles—enough to sail from Nazi-occupied France to the Gulf of Mexico, prowl for a while and return.[236]

The two Type IX U-boats arrived at the mouth of the Mississippi on May 10 and began their "merry massacre."[237] For eleven days, the U-boats set about their work attacking merchant ships, including the SS *Heredia*. An anecdote from one of the attacks shows the morbid sense of humor the German crewmen showed toward the survivors of their attacks. After sinking the American freighter *Norlindo*, the Germans gave the survivors of the ship "40 packs of cigarettes, a cake with French writing, crackers, matches, water, and ten gallons of lime pulp made from fresh limes," and told them, "Sorry we can't help you. Hope you get ashore OK." In a

U.S. Coast Guard watching depth charge explosion from stern of USCGC *Spencer*, 1943. *From Library of Congress.*

throwback to the pirate Jean Lafitte's time, the crew of U-507 fired on, boarded and scuttled a Honduran freighter south of Barataria Bay, where Lafitte himself had once hunted. For eleven days, the two U-boats harried ships in the area, sinking seven.

In total, the two U-boats sank seventeen ships on their voyage to and from the mouth of the Mississippi, killing two hundred crewmen. The toll might have been much higher if not for the fact that nine of U-507's fourteen torpedoes missed or malfunctioned. Having exhausted their torpedoes, the crews of the two U-boats headed back for Europe via Florida.[238]

In all, twenty-six ships were attacked at the mouth of the Mississippi from May to July 1942, and another sixteen sunk. A total of forty-one ships were sunk in the Gulf Sea Frontier, which included the Caribbean, during that time period. May 1942 earned the Gulf Sea Frontier the grim distinction of having the highest number of ships sunk in any area in the war in a single month.[239]

DENTON W. CROCKER STOOD on the rear platform of his Pullman train in the August heat, taking in the scenery. He saw swampland, cypress trees and Spanish moss. He had gotten his first look at south Louisiana, where he would be spending the next five months learning how to beat malaria. A few hours later, he was riding in an army truck "in style" down Canal Street. He marveled at the ironwork of the French Quarter and—always the biologist—took special note of the palm trees that gave the city a "very southern appearance."[240]

Crocker was taken to the barracks at Camp Plauche, where he noticed that standing water in front of the building was alive with mosquito larvae. As his training began, he realized that the antimalaria units were so new that they were largely unorganized, and instruction might be lacking. That fact might have flummoxed another soldier, but Crocker relished the freedom to learn outside the classroom. Within days of arriving at Camp Plauche, Crocker had already started a collection of slide-mounted mosquito larvae and had begun a log of "biting records."[241]

At Camp Plauche, Crocker showed not only his unquenchable curiosity but also an unflagging optimism. Crocker and his fellow soldiers slept in their un-airconditioned barracks on beds without sheets or blankets. Rather than complain, Crocker noted that making the bed in the morning was much easier. "I can understand the slowness of southerners now," he wrote in a letter to his parents back home, "for the least movement brings torrents of perspiration." There were so many cockroaches in their barracks at night that the sound of them moving was like "the ticking of a clock." Rather than show disgust at the invaders, Crocker wrote that the "little tykes" helped him sleep peacefully.[242]

As Crocker had first suspected when he arrived at Camp Plauche, his classes on malaria control were somewhat less than revelatory. He had already learned on his own much of the content of the classes and found himself again taking on the role of teacher. He was delighted when the other men in his unit showed genuine interest in the minute details of plasmodium anatomy. Crocker continued his independent studies outside of class. His superiors told him and the other antimalaria men to "tell nobody about the things we study here." This command underscored the potential advantage defeating malaria would grant in a conflict with the Japanese. If Allied soldiers in the Pacific could defeat the disease, they'd be effectively tripling their manpower.[243]

Crocker and his fellow soldiers often received permission to travel into New Orleans, and they found plenty to do in the city, though the way Crocker spent his time was very different from the way some other soldiers did. New Orleans, he noted, was a "wide open town," and the men who spent time there came back to camp with wild stories. Drinking to excess, of course, was rampant, and "sex immorality" was a problem too. Soldiers, both single and married, found themselves succumbing to temptation and sleeping with women who Crocker described as "a poor bunch...doubtless infected with disease."[244]

Crocker was much more interested in culture, history and food, spending his days in New Orleans cruising the Mississippi River on a steamboat, visiting the natural history museum and the zoo and admiring historic buildings like the Cabildo and Old Absinthe House. A lover of fruit, Croker would take notes on the individual pieces of fruit that he found and consumed on his voyage through the Pacific. He bought watermelon slices at a fruit stand and beignets and coffee from Morning Call. A large man and self-described "chow hound," Crocker delighted in the city's fine-dining restaurants, eating lavish meals at Antoine's and Tujagues. He was drawn to seafood dishes, ordering the shrimp à la creole multiple times at Antoine's. Once, after eating a dish of broiled crab, Crocker bragged about how he "was even able to identify the crab."[245]

Though Crocker was enjoying his time spent in New Orleans, a constant uneasiness hung over him and his fellow soldiers. When he arrived in New

Orleans, he had no idea when he would be deployed or where he would go. His best guess was that he'd spend a month or two in the city and then head for India or China. In addition to his classes, Crocker marched regularly through the marshy areas surrounding New Orleans and underwent frequent drills and inspections. Most of Crocker's letters home, which he published later in life, are lighthearted and full of details about the flora and fauna of Louisiana and the Pacific and professions of love for Jean-Marie, the woman who would become his wife. But underneath the optimism and lightheartedness were clues that Crocker was in for hard times. "There are more doggone inspections here than I have ever seen before," he wrote to his parents. "Of course, it is essential to go overseas with everything in good condition because when something gives out in the jungle somewhere it can be serious."[246]

Although Crocker was forbidden from writing to his parents and fiancée about the details of his training, decades later he would publish a scholarly article about the strategies he and his compatriots employed in fighting mosquitoes and malaria in the Pacific theater. Of the two types of antimalaria units being trained at Camp Plauche—survey units and control units—Crocker was a member of a survey unit. His job overseas would be primarily to put his scientific mind to use studying mosquitoes and their habitats. He was tasked with figuring out which mosquitoes lived where and recommending methods for control. He would monitor the effectiveness of the control measures, constantly gathering data on how many mosquitoes were around and how many carried the malaria parasite. Crocker's antimalaria unit would travel in a series of tents, which held not only the men but also their lab equipment and trunks of literature.[247]

For the final six weeks of Crocker's stay in New Orleans, he moved to Jackson Barracks in the Lower Ninth Ward. From there, he would proceed to deployment. Although he was "utterly bored" during that time, it did give him a chance to further explore New Orleans. Crocker and his friend Bill Brown would make fake passes to get out of the barracks, and they always headed for the French Quarter. Brown was a jazz fan, and they would pub crawl through the Quarter, drinking and listening to music. In his memoir, Crocker gives a vivid snapshot of what the bars of the French Quarter were like in those weeks:

> *I have an image of one very large black woman…sitting at a piano, playing and singing for hours it seemed. The streets swarmed both with service men and civilians and the noisy bars, opening onto the street, had people flowing*

into and out of them. As we passed by we could look in and I remember one place where a nearly naked woman was gyrating wildly up on the bar, her high heels clicking out the beat of the music. Her only clothing was a flap of cloth, about the size of a 50 cent piece, which with an occasional thrust of the hips she could flip up, rendering her completely naked.[248]

He was experiencing the city to the fullest, and he would soon take his memories of New Orleans with him to the Pacific. Within a month of the wild nights out in the French Quarter, Crocker was finally told it was time to leave. On January 25, 1944, Crocker and the other members of his antimalaria unit marched from their barracks to Chalmette Slip where they boarded the SS *Mexico*. They spent a night anchored in the Mississippi River, then headed for the Gulf the following day. Crocker watched flocks of brown and white pelicans as he left the Mississippi and the United States.

As Denton W. Crocker's ship sailed into the open Gulf, the men aboard beheld a comforting sight—another troop transport, with two imposing U.S. Navy destroyers (one a small, fast "subchaser" and one a larger ship) and a Catalina PBY "flying boat" (an American airplane that would earn a reputation as an effective tool of anti-submarine warfare). Crocker and his compatriots were part of a convoy. They had also entered the hunting grounds of the U-boats.[249]

But things were very different in January 1944, than they had been a year and a half earlier, when the Nazi submarine packs had shed so much blood in the Gulf. Though the United States had been caught off guard by the submarine attacks of 1942, it had rapidly and forcefully adapted. Historian Samuel Eliot Morison likened defeating Hitler's submarine fleets to "lifting an immense jellyfish. Grasping it with two hands accomplished nothing, but with hands-all-around and heaving together, one could really do something to the so-and-so." The many hands that contributed to defeating the submarine threat were the navies of the United States, Britain, Canada and Brazil; other branches of the U.S. forces; the Merchant Marine; civilian scientists and lawmakers; and the general public. Cooperation was required all around.

Crocker was given a taste of how effective the U.S. Navy's antisubmarine tactics had become when, at 3:00 a.m. on the first night in the Gulf, alarms sounded, flares were launched and crews manned their guns. It turned out to be a false alarm, but if a U-boat had been in the area, it would have faced hellfire from the destroyers.[250]

Sailors detonating depth charges off the bow of their cutter. *From Library of Congress.*

The convoy itself was a means of combating U-boats—grouping ships together in traveling packs meant that planes and destroyers had a much smaller area to patrol and defend. Allied forces also developed new and improved weapons to combat U-boats, including better depth charges and antisubmarine-specific weapons such as the "hedgehog," a rocket-loaded battery that could pepper the water with dozens of small charges. Radar helped ship crews detect U-boats. Two of the most effective tools that the Allies used to defeat the U-boats were present at the mouth of the Mississippi when Crocker and his antimalaria men sailed into the Gulf. These were the small, fast subchaser destroyer and specialist airplanes that could not only spot and attack U-boats (more than 40 percent of all U-boats sunk during the war were sunk by Catalina PBYs like the one escorting Crocker)[251] but also land and refuel in water.[252]

By the time Crocker and his unit sailed through the Gulf, the tide had turned against the U-boat. The Allies' antisubmarine tactics had worked, and dozens of U-boats had been sunk in 1943. Allied shipping was far more organized, denying the U-boats the surprise and isolation they needed to be effective. The Nazis privately wondered whether they should give up their U-boat strategy altogether. They decided to continue trying to sink as many Allied ships as possible but never approached the success they had enjoyed early in the war.[253]

Denton Crocker would sail through the Panama Canal to New Guinea, where he set about conducting the science that would turn out to be crucial for the United States' victory in the Pacific. He traveled for two years, following the Japanese retreat to the Spice Islands, Philippines, Okinawa and finally Japan. He survived kamikaze attacks by the Japanese but lived to tell his story, marry Jean-Marie and live a long and productive life as an academic in the Northeast. His antimalaria unit—the Thirty-First Malaria Survey Unit—became known as one of the most effective malaria units to serve overseas.[254]

New Orleans had felt the sting of Hitler's *Paukenschlag* early in the war, but by 1944, the city had shown that a submarine assault would not close its port. It had shown that it would do its part in winning the war against the Axis powers by training the mosquito fighters who would clear the air ahead of island-hopping Allied troops.

A Catalina "Flying Boat" aircraft patrols near Singapore. *From Library of Congress.*

10

Lavender Line

Tennessee Williams and Gay New Orleans

And it was even the year when I usually had what the French call "papillons d'amour" because I did not have the price of a bottle of Cuprex, the standard pubic pesticide in those days, and when I was once embarrassed by this outcry on a crowded street corner in daylight, 'You bastard, you gave me crabs last night!"—an outcry which cut short my social season in the French Quarter of New Orleans and sent me packing—well, packing is hardly the word, since I had no luggage—on my thumb to Florida.[255]
—*Tennessee Williams,* Memoirs

Art imitates life. Tennessee Williams's life in New Orleans lends plenty of weight to this claim. He frequently drew on the endless living art that is New Orleans for his plays. The exotic city offered him the opportunity to create characters so flamboyant, so flawed, so human, so New Orleans.

This beloved New Orleans writer captured the beauty, ambiance and mysteries of the Crescent City. And its gayness. It was a time of confusion and solidarity, of pride and fear and of sex and parties. Gay New Orleans of the 1940s, '50s, '60s and '70s was a well-known secret.

The life of Tennessee Williams—and the lives of his characters—paralleled the history of New Orleans for three decades.

At 722 Rue Toulouse was a cramped, dingy house with a witch of a landlady. Its residents complained constantly about the roaches, the lightbulbs that were never replaced, and the damp walls. But they had no choice but to pay the rent and endure another month. And another. And another. They were the destitute of New Orleans. One might even say they were the norm of New Orleans.

The writer lived upstairs, at least for a few more days. He had just pawned his typewriter and the last of his clothes, minus the pants and faded red flannel he had on. He lay in bed, anxious for the future, trying desperately to sleep.

The consumptive painter next door entered the writer's room and sat next to him on the bed. "You don't seem experienced yet…kid, are you…excuse my blunt approach…but are you?" The writer froze as the stranger put his hand on his sheet-covered body. "Ain't come out completely, as we put it?" The writer explained that he had just one experience in St. Louis. He had met an army man at a party and allowed himself to be used. When he told the soldier he loved him, he flew out the following morning, leaving behind no way in which to reach him.

The painter crawled into bed next to the stunned and nervous writer. He told him to relax and imagine the soldier. An hour later, the writer sat on the edge of his cot, bundled in his sheet and smoking a cigarette. He was wondering what his grandmother would say if she had been privy to the last hour.

Even in his increasingly frequent drunken states, even in his drug-induced stupors, Tye was a devilishly handsome man with a godlike body. His ole lady and roommate, Jane, was head over heels in love with him. So was the painter. And the writer was fast becoming so.

Tye worked in the Quarter as a barker for a Bourbon Street Strip Club. He was also a thief, a womanizer and an addict. But no one seemed to care—he was that good-looking and charming.

One night, he stumbled his way home, climbed the stairs of 722 Rue Toulouse and collapsed outside his door. The writer helped him onto his own cot and got his wet shoes off. "Shoes? Yes, but nothin' else. Once I—passed out on—Bourbon Street—late night—in a dark doorway—woke up—this guy, was takin' liberties with me and I don't go for that stuff—" and then he fell into a drunken sleep. The writer passed the consumptive painter in the hall and walked downstairs to the kitchen. He sat with the landlady while she made a pot of gumbo.

Moments later, an angry shout reached the kitchen. "Hey! Whatcha doin'? Git yuh fuckin' hands off me!"

"I thought I was visiting a friend."

"'Sthat how you visit a friend, unzippin' his pants an' pullin' out his dick?....No goddam faggot messes with me, never! For lessn' a hundred dollars!"

Tye stumbled out of the writer's cubicle and into the arms of Jane, who led him to their room. The two promptly began making love. The painter waited for the writer to crawl into his cot and then stood suggestive and smoking in the doorway. He was sent away. The writer ran his hands dreamily up and down his cot along the warm human indentation that had been Tye.

Jane awoke and noticed the needle mark on Tye's arm. His silky-smooth skin had felt good on her own last night. It always did. But the needle mark, combined with the traces of lipstick smeared on his face and other parts, convinced her that their extended liaison must end.

Besides, she was dying. She had gotten the news from Oschner's a few days ago. Her condition, which seemed to have gone into remission upon meeting Tye, was back. She didn't have very long, and she had some loose ends to take care of.

Then there was the Brazilian millionaire who had mistaken her for a high-dollar whore at the Blue Lantern a few nights ago. The portly gentleman had offered her a $100 bill. She refused but took his business card. The hole in the arm and lipstick convinced Jane to call her suitor and leave a message at the Hotel Royal Orleans: "Senorita Bonita of the Blue Lantern awaits you, top floor of seven-two-two Toulouse."

Tye's prowess in bed offered her plenty of distractions from her condition. But the Brazilian had money.

The painter was also dying—faster than Jane. Like Jane, he was getting all the sex he could before that final separation of body and soul. He was accustomed to bringing young men to his room. There were always the desperate delinquents of the Quarter who would sell their bodies for a warm bed. And there had been that night with the writer. He wished there had been more nights with the writer. Now he was coughing the last of his lifeblood out on his cot, unable to even think about gratifying his lust.

Knowing that the painter was soon to be forcibly removed from 722 Toulouse, the writer stopped by his cot to pay his final respects. He offered to phone a private doctor who would insist that the dying man not be moved, but the painter declared, "My faith's in Christ—not doctors." The religious profession shocked the writer, and he said so.

The consumptive continued, "I'm a Catholic believer. A priest would say that you have fallen from Grace, boy." He combed his hair delicately and put on makeup as if he had an amorous night planned. "If necessary, I'll go into *Sanctuary*!"

When the Writer laughed, he exclaimed, "Joke, is it, is it a joke?! Foxes have holes, but the Son of Man hath nowhere to hide his head!" Recognizing his delirium and understanding his inevitable fate, the writer suggested that he take more than his usual dose of sleeping pills. "Why, you're suggesting suicide to me which is a cardinal sin, would put me in unhallowed ground in—potter's field. I believe in God the Father, God the Son, and God the Holy Ghost."

Unable to help, the writer unscrewed the bottle of pills, left them on the bed stand and went back to his own cubicle.[256]

TENNESSEE WILLIAMS ARRIVED IN New Orleans on December 28, 1938. After a few hours wandering the Quarter, he returned to his room and wrote, "Here surely is a place I was made for if any place on this funny old world."[257] One week later, he moved into 722 Toulouse Street, where he signed in as "Tennessee Williams—Writer." He would spend three weeks in that dingy house—three weeks that would haunt him but also fill him with nostalgia for the remainder of his life.

When his play, *Vieux Carre*, came out in 1977, Williams told a reporter that "the events in the house did actually take place….There are two characters in it, a boy and a girl, whom I knew later in another house, not in that one. But all the others were there at 722 Toulouse Street, in 1939."[258]

Thomas Lanier Williams was born in Columbus, Mississippi. He spent his formative years in St. Louis. He lived in New York City. He owned a house and vacationed in Key West. He went to Rome whenever he could. He dreamed of retiring on a goat farm in Sicily. But it was New Orleans that he called his spiritual home.

He loved the food, the balmy atmosphere, the freedom, the bohemian lifestyle and the nightlife. But most of all, he loved the Lavender Line.

New Orleans had been a haven for homosexuals for the past half century.

THE UNDERFED BUT SEDUCTIVE young man stood outside the house on 1014 Dumaine Street. It was five o'clock in the morning, and Williams had been at work for half an hour. He planned to write for several more. After buzzing the youth in the front gate, the writer explained that he needed to work and asked if the appointment could be rescheduled for eight o'clock. The young man agreed, and Williams went back to work, trying to balance two of his passions—writing and sex.

Williams had met the young man the night before at a Bourbon Street club on Lavender Line. The club promised to assuage his desires. The youth's name was Lyle, and he immediately attracted the older man's attention. According to Williams, "The boys wear G-strings only—so you can be pretty sure what you're getting. I would recommend, however, that penetration be avoided, as they are most probably all infected with clap in the ass. And I'd also recommend that you get them to bathe as their hours are long and sweaty. And that you have a pubic pesticide such as A-200."[259]

Williams always seemed to find a lover when the mood struck him. The worst the writer ever received was a jilted heart and an occasional, treatable sexually transmitted disease. Others were not so fortunate.

Fernando Rios was walking down Pere Antoine Alley, and so were three students from Tulane University—John S. Farrell, Alberto A. Calvo and David P. Drennan. Rather, one was walking with Rios, while two waited in ambush.

Fernando had spent the evening at a gay bar, Café Lafitte in Exile. He was looking for love or at least a lay. The three students were also looking for a gay man—to assault.

Fernando was a visiting tour guide who was leading a group of affluent Mexican doctors and their wives through New Orleans. Earlier that day, he had led his charges to the Presbytère, the Cabildo and St. Louis Cathedral, with its two famous side alleys, Pirate's Alley and Pere Antoine Alley, one that honored an outlaw the other a beloved priest. Fernando would visit the latter again later that night.

After the tour concluded that Saturday, September 27, 1958, the five-foot-ten, 143-pound Fernando left his company at the Roosevelt Hotel and headed toward Bourbon Street for some personal time. He ended up at Café Lafitte in Exile, where he met John Farrell at about 1:30 a.m. Not long after, the two were strolling down Pere Antoine Alley. Suddenly, Farrell turned on him and began beating him savagely. Calvo and Drennan immediately came to assist him.

Moments later, the three students were headed back to Tulane, and Fernando lay on the cool pavement with multiple skull fractures, hemorrhages, facial lacerations, a subdural hematoma and damage to the lungs, heart, and liver.

Two days later, the three students turned themselves in to the police. Facing homicide and robbery charges (they had taken Fernando's wallet with forty dollars' worth of pesos and Canadian and American dollars), their defense was that they had been sexually propositioned by "a pervert Mexican, medical freak with an eggshell cranium."

Four months later, the trio was acquitted. The packed courtroom began cheering when the jury announced their decision. Apparently, Fernando was punched when he "made an improper advance" on Farrell. He fell to the ground, and his unusually thin cranium cracked.

The message to gay New Orleans was loud and clear.[260]

WILLIAMS WOULD RISE EARLY, drink black coffee and immediately get to work. Most days he would spend four or five hours hard at work. The rest of the day was his. And there was plenty to occupy a bon vivant in New Orleans. Most nights ended with a man in his bed—either one of his long-term boyfriends or a temporary fling. If needed, there were always the boys at the club or a prostitute. One way or another, he would have company.

Day after day, month after month, year after year passed thusly. Tennessee Williams was living the life he felt he needed to for the sake of his vocation. As he said, "What is my profession but living and putting it all down in stories and plays and now in this book?"[261] All the debauchery was for the sake of his work: "Work!!—the loveliest of all four-letter words, surpassing even the importance of love, most times."[262] Not even a weakened heart caused by too much drinking or venereal disease stopped the writer. No, he would write and live until the very end. As he believed, "How sad a thing for an artist to abandon his art: I think it's much sadder than death."[263]

New Orleans inspired a number of Williams's most famous works. *A Streetcar Named Desire*, *Suddenly Last Summer*, *Vieux Carre* and *Something Unspoken*, to name a few, were written in or about New Orleans. He wrote these and other works, including much of his *Memoirs* at a number of locales in the Quarter, including 722 Toulouse Street, 632½ St. Peter Street, the Hotel Maison de Ville at 727 Toulouse Street, the Hotel Monteleone at 214 Royal Street and 1014 Dumaine Street.

He drew on other sources of inspiration at a number of his favorite haunts in the Quarter—Galatoire's, Marti's and Brennan's. And, of course, there were the gay bars, including Café Lafitte in Exile.

Café Lafitte in Exile, the oldest continuously operating gay bar in the United States, open twenty-four hours at 901 Bourbon Street in the French Quarter of New Orleans. *From Creative Commons.*

WITH HIS ATTRACTION TO the gay bars of the Quarter, it is a bit surprising that the playwright was never arrested during any of the sporadic and frequent raids by the vice police. He was also lucky that he was not at the Upstairs Lounge the night of June 24, 1973.

Rodger Dale Nunez was being unceremoniously dragged through the Upstairs Lounge on the corner of Chartres and Iberville Streets. As he was being shoved into the open air, he shouted that he would "burn you all out."

Thirty minutes later, the front of the Upstairs Lounge erupted in flames. The bartender led about twenty patrons out of a poorly marked fire exit. Others ran to the windows, only to find themselves trapped by the burglar bars. One skinny man, already aflame, squeezed through the bars and fell to his death on the concrete below. The rest burned alive, including Reverend Bill Larson, who was found charred and wedged between the bars—his face and one arm hanging lifeless over the street.

Minutes later, the fire department arrived. It was too late for twenty-eight of the patrons. Four more would die of injuries in the coming days.

The June 24, 1973 burning of the Upstairs Lounge was a tragedy. But it was not a homophobic crime. It was a spat between two gay men that turned deadly. The aftermath, however, would show how most of New Orleans viewed the gay community.

Many of the deceased remained unidentified by their "loved" ones, and most churches refused to offer their facilities for a memorial service. Some even suggested that the "queers be buried in fruit jars." Only one pastor, Episcopal priest Bill Richardson, stepped forward and offered the use of St. George's Episcopal Church to memorialize the dead.[264]

WHEN HE WASN'T CRUISING the bar scene, Tennessee was often found entertaining at his own place. More often than not, these entertainments were the exclusive affair of him and his boyfriend—or whoever was fulfilling that role on a particular evening. Other times, the soirees involved a handful of intimate New Orleans characters.

The drinking, socializing and sex kept the playwright going, but not all gatherings were equally enjoyable. One of Tennessee Williams's first New Orleans parties ended abruptly and uncomfortably, but at least it provided a footnote in *Memoirs*.

When the famous playwright first moved to New Orleans, he was courted by the elite—mostly the Garden District variety. One evening, he decided to return the favor and host them at his own Quarter apartment on Orleans Street. In the midst of the party, a young woman asked Tennessee if she could see his bedroom. He acquiesced.

> *"He's going to show us his bedroom!" exclaimed the young lady. The whole party trooped in. They seemed to like the bedroom....Then somebody turned to my apartment mate. "Now show us yours." He probably knew that scandal was brewing and would have wished to avoid it but I found it perfectly natural to say, "We share this room." I thought the silence that followed my statement was not natural at all. You see the bed was somewhere between single and double.*

Soon after, the young ladies and their escorts began to thank Tennessee two by two and depart for their Uptown homes.[265]

ANOTHER SMALL GATHERING AMONG friends had just as inauspicious a start as Williams's failed Uptown party. Yet the former soirée would soon turn into one of the nation's largest festivals.

The largest gay celebration in New Orleans is Southern Decadence. The festival, which now brings in more than 130,000 visitors and $160 million, sprang from the humblest of beginnings.

Maureen had come to New Orleans by way of Manhattan. She was staying with friends in a former slave quarters in Treme, 2110 Barracks Street. The roommates jokingly called their meager housing *Belle Reve* in honor of Blanche DuBois's plantation in Tennessee Williams's *A Streetcar Named Desire*. The move to New Orleans had thus far been underwhelming for Maureen. It was hot. There was nothing to do. Maureen's roommates decided to throw a party. On the Sunday before Labor Day in 1972, the friends—black, white, straight, gay—threw a themed party. They were to come dressed as their favorite southern decadents. Costumed impersonators of Tallulah Bankhead, Belle Watling and Mary Ann Mobley were among the revelers that Labor Day.[266]

The Southern Decadence Parade was one of the pivotal moments in New Orleans's gay history, at least politically speaking. Frank Perez explains, "The success of Southern Decadence revealed to the straight community in New Orleans the spending power of the gay community long before the rest of the country realized that gay people were a powerful economic market with loads of expendable income."

Inevitably, one politician after another began to realize, however gradually, the economic and political value of the disproportionately large number of gays in their community. While it was previously believed that tourist dollars required the padlocking of the proverbial gay closet, the spending power of the gay community was beginning to contribute to its social acceptance.[267]

⌐--···--⌐

WILLIAMS GREW UP WITH a keen understanding of human mortality. He lived most of his life with heart problems, a cataract in his left eye and depression that was self-treated with alcohol. He lived his whole life convinced that he had only a short time to make his mark. He viewed each passing year as a year survived, icing on the cake and one year closer to the day when his failing heart would inevitably explode. When that day came, he hoped it would be in New Orleans: "I hope to die in my sleep, when the time comes, and I hope it will be in the beautiful big

Andy Warhol (*left*) and Tennessee Williams (*right*) talking on the SS *France*, 1967. *World Journal Tribune photo by James Kavallines, from Library of Congress.*

brass bed in my New Orleans apartment, the bed which is associated with so much love."[268]

Die, he did. But alas, it would not be in New Orleans. Instead, he died after choking on a plastic medicine top in a New York City hotel suite on February 25, 1983. He was thirteen hundred miles from his beloved New Orleans.[269]

FORTUNATELY, SHOCKINGLY AND SOME would say miraculously, Williams lived to a respectable age, active and coherent until the end. Many of his gay comrades could not say the same. As Tennessee's sexual liaisons were on the decline, the plague hit.

AIDS devastated the gay community of New Orleans (and Miami and New York and everywhere) with deadly proficiency. A longtime bartender at Café Lafitte in Exile summed up the effects of the deadly disease on the Quarter:

It was so bad you were afraid to answer your phone. I remember throwing away my address book because most everyone in it had died. It was horrible. No one knew what was going on and everyone was fearful. Charity Hospital had a separate floor for AIDS patients. Orderlies would set patient's meals outside the doors in the hall for fear of being in the same room with someone infected. And visitors were forced to wear masks and gowns. You'd go to the hospital to visit a friend and be shocked at how sickly they looked but also at how many other people you knew were also patients. After a while it took a heavy toll on me. I became cold.[270]

Because New Orleans was a tourist destination, the virus spread rapidly. Many believed the disease to be the just reward for a fallen lifestyle. However, unlike the reaction to the 1973 Upstairs Lounge fire, many in New Orleans began to sympathize with the stricken community. Attorney Jack Sullivan saw a silver lining behind the epidemic: "AIDS forced so many people out of the closet, the mainstream establishment realized, 'Oh, I didn't know you were gay.' AIDS created a forced visibility." In short, it humanized the gay community in the eyes of many New Orleanians.[271]

In 1993, Louisiana enacted a domestic partnership ordinance. Six years later, the state's sodomy law was struck down. Gays in New Orleans won more freedoms and more tolerance, and their culture began to thrive in an unprecedented atmosphere of acceptance.

At the close of the second decade of the third millennium, the gay community in New Orleans has more visibility, power and culture than perhaps anywhere in the nation. New Orleans has become the Elysium that Tennessee Williams and so many like him sought.

II

GUMBO

Vignettes from New Orleans's Food History

1700

Pierre Le Moyne d'Iberville looked over the side of his chaloupe at the east bank of the Mississippi. *That's a good spot for a fort*, he thought. *I'll have to remember that when I come back down river.*

Iberville was touring the Mississippi with Andre Penicaut, who by now was something of a veteran. He'd been up the Mississippi twice already. The men rowed by what would become the French Quarter and New Orleans. There was nothing to note then. It was just wilderness.

A few miles north of the future site of New Orleans, Iberville met the Bayagoula Indians for the first time. The Bayagoula ran into the woods, but with a little coaxing from the Frenchmen's Biloxi companion, they emerged, peace pipe in hand. Iberville smoked from the pipe and ate a little of the Bayagoula's food—flour mixed with cold water, some bread and fish. *Did you get enough to eat?* The Bayagoula asked. *Do you need women?*

The Frenchmen left after three days, loaded down with a "great number" of fowl the Indians had killed. Their little spot along the Mississippi was great for hunting birds. A few of the Bayagoula went with them. They traveled a little farther north to Istrouma (Baton Rouge), which marked the boundary between the Bayagoula and the Shakchi Humma. The Shakchi Humma, who would come to be known by Europeans simply as the Houma, used a feisty little red crustacean called the crawfish for their war emblem.[272]

1718

A young woman stood looking at the sad little encampment on the Mississippi. Jean-Baptiste Le Moyne de Bienville, governor of Louisiana, and a party of forty or so rough men were working to carve the city of New Orleans out of the wilderness. In those days, New Orleans was still mostly dense canebrake with swampy soil and standing water everywhere. The woman looked over the buildings of the settlement; they were all made of logs.

I know what these men need, the woman thought. *These men need oysters.* The young woman who would become known only as "Madam Bangs" began hauling loads of oysters to the young town from the faraway Pascagoula River in present-day Mississippi. The journey from the Pascagoula to New Orleans would take her through Mississippi Sound, Lake Borgne, the Rigolets, Lake Pontchartrain, Bayou St. John and finally to the city. She hauled her cargo of oysters to the city so many times that she became a master sailor.

Word of Madam Bangs spread on the frontier, and her sailing skill grew legendary. "He is as good a sailor as Madam Bangs," frontier people would say when someone was particularly good at sailing. Madam Bangs was said to be 120 when she finally died in the early 1800s. God only knows how many oysters she carried to New Orleans in all those years.[273]

1727

Water. That's all she wanted. No, not she, but we. That's what her vows accustomed her to say. Nevertheless, water!

"There were already days in which we were reduced to a pint of water per day….We suffered much from thirst, and that made us exchange our wine for water; however they only gave us a bottle of water for a bottle of wine. Even then, we were happy to have water at that price." Little did Sister Madeleine Hachard realize what a vital role water would play in the history of her new home. It was the source of life. It was a source of destruction.

New Orleans is surrounded by water—the Mississippi River, Lake Pontchartrain, the swamps to the south, water below (in 1819, engineer Benjamin Henry Latrobe hit water just three feet below the surface), and, frequently, water from above. Water is such a constant presence and threat that the dead are buried above ground. Houses are built on pilings that go fifty feet into the earth. Every third year, New Orleans is one inch lower. Two-fifths of all the water in the continental United States flows by the Crescent City on its way to the Gulf. In effect, it is a bowl surrounded by water. And the water is getting higher each year.

Exactly two hundred years after Marie and her fellow Ursulines arrived, a storm poured fourteen inches of water on the city, causing the storm drains to fail. One week later, a tanker crashed into the levee wall and a sixty-foot crevasse appeared, threatening to drown the city. Seventy-eight years later, another levee broke. Again, water poured into the city, this time killing around one thousand people.

But in 1727, all Sister Madeleine wanted was a glass.[274]

1730

The recently freed slave sat in his house, tired from the day's events. He had made several livres for flogging a white man, then he had made forty more when he broke another man's four limbs, hips and thighs and left him on the wheel, face upward, to fry in the summer sun.

Now he sat at table awaiting his wife's meal. He was glad he had her as the scent of the meal filled his nostrils—a spiced roux that she had been constantly stirring for more than an hour, fresh sausage and the okra he had loved so much as a child in Africa. He knew she had thrown in extra okra, as so many slave and Creole wives did, for it was the okra that made the dish.

Louis Congo had been a slave since 1721 when his ship landed in Biloxi. He was sold to a master in New Orleans but had since earned his freedom. He earned his livelihood by beating, torturing and executing the condemned of New Orleans—black and white alike.

He had a few more floggings and a hanging to enforce tomorrow. But for now, he sat back and enjoyed the flavorful bowl of gumbo his wife had put before him.[275]

1819

Henry Bradshaw Fearon was on a mission. The Englishman had been tasked by friends back home with exploring the young United States and reporting back on the suitability of the country for emigration. He had traveled all over, and while the abolitionist didn't think his friends would consider moving to New Orleans, he didn't want to ignore the city.

He left Natchez on the steamboat *Orleans* and headed south. He passed well-built houses and sugar plantations on the outskirts of New Orleans, then was delighted by the sight of the many ships' masts bristling at the port. After exploring the small towns of the county's frontier, he had finally arrived at a true city.

He arrived on a Sunday and noted that the Sabbath day had not kept the city from buzzing. He was particularly struck by how much New Orleanians liked to gamble. Coffeehouses were filled from morning to night with gamblers. "It is said that when the Kentuckians arrive at this place they are in their glory," he wrote, "finding neither limit to, nor punishment of their excesses."

Fearon marveled at the luxury of Davis's Hotel and chuckled at an exhibition called "Furious Animals," which pitted tigers, bulls, bears and dogs against one another. After seeing a play, Fearon went to a pub, where he saw a man stabbed. "These things are of every day occurrence," he wrote. "It is not often that they are taken cognizance of by police."

Food in the city was of poor quality and expensive, he wrote. But he was more concerned with securing the staples of home—English ham and cheese, Irish beef and butter—than with sampling the native cuisine of the city.

All in all, Fearon wrote to his friends at home, "To live a short life but a merry one, I have no hesitation in recommending New Orleans."[276]

1838

The Poydras Street Market was booming. Money—a lot of it—was changing hands. The Second Municipality needed its cut. This was the United States, after all.

For all of New Orleans's history, the French and Spanish had controlled the city. But now, English-speaking Americans did. At least a chunk of the city. New Orleans had been divided into three municipalities, and the English speakers could govern the Second Municipality as they liked. The First and Third Municipalities were still controlled by the French speakers.

The French had been happy to allow the Poydras Street Market to operate in such a messy and untaxed way, but the commissioners of the Second

The Poydras Street Market. *From Library of Congress.*

Municipality had fixed that. From now on, anyone wanting to sell food in the Poydras Street Market would have to give the municipality its share. For every cow sold, the municipality would get eighty-seven and a half cents. For every pig, calf, sheep or deer, twenty-five cents. Fish mongers could rent a table for twelve and a half cents. The market would be the place for buying fish, shrimp, crab, crawfish, turtles and game—the only place (enforceable by penalty of five to fifteen dollars).

Of course, rules were good. Since the English-speakers had officially taken control of the Second Municipality, commerce had thrived. The long list of rules the Second Municipality was enacting for the Poydras Street Market would make it a much nicer place to shop. Butchers would have their own little corner of the market and fishmongers theirs. Vegetable sellers would be set apart from fruit sellers. It would be more organized. And to make things safer, the market would be chained off, so no carriages could come through during business hours, which would be strictly set and enforced. The chain gangs would clean.

Yes, the Poydras Market was about to change for the better. It was about to be Americanized.[277]

161

1841

R.F. Nichols paced the aisles of his store on Camp Street, making note of all the sweet, salty, crunchy, chewy, intoxicating and invigorating sundries he could offer to his fellow New Orleanians: enough Smyrna figs to feed an army; raisins, grapes, jams, jellies and strawberries in syrup; nearly one thousand boxes of sardines; and pickles, macaroni and butter crackers. A person could host a Roman feast with a stop by his store. *Cigars—must mention the cigars.* His pen scribbled out "20,000 Spanish Segars."

Then there was the booze. Nichols could get the whole city drunk. He had more than one thousand bottles of old English port, plenty of Baltimore gin, six hundred bottles of sherry and another twenty-four hundred bottles of sweet liqueurs of all type. He had two hundred boxes of claret wine, and then there was the bounce—the cherry bounce. Nichols had fifty barrels of the stuff, with all of those sour little mashed-up cherries floating in liquor. Ah, the good times all that cherry bounce would facilitate.

He looked over his inventory. *I am rich in delicious things*, he thought, *and when I sell all these things, I'll be rich in money! Or* richer, *I should say.*

Nichols finished his list and set off for the *Daily Picayune*. He couldn't wait for people to read about all of the delicious things.[278]

1862

"Coffee $1. Per pound, and Ma has notified us that we must soon say 'good bye' to it. She tried the experiment of mixing it with rye, but we were dissatisfied with it." Clara Solomon was not pleased. Coffee, a New Orleans staple, was in short supply. The Beast had seen to that.

Coffee had been a New Orleans staple for more than one hundred years when the Civil War erupted. A French culture coupled with easy access to the French Caribbean coffee plantations assured that coffee would be the preferred drink of New Orleanians, as opposed to tea, which was preferred by those up north. Yet tea had taken a hit during the Revolutionary War and the taxes that preceded it. Coffee had become the drink of choice. By 1840, New Orleans was the nation's second leading importer of coffee.

"Coffee is $1.25 a pound, and Ma and Mrs. N. have both determined not to have it, and for the first time in many years, coffee will not to be on our breakfast table. Ma is going to get some Cocoa. I shall miss it very much."

A waiter presents a cup of chicory coffee. *From Library of Congress.*

The Union blockade of New Orleans forced residents to seek ways to make their coffee last. They turned to acorns, beets and chicory. Eventually, coffee under any guise became a delicacy.

"Breakfast will soon be ready. No coffee! No coffee!"

Coffee is still consumed in copious amounts by New Orleanians, chicory included. Millions of tourists visit the Crescent City each year, and most make a stop at Café du Monde where they imbibe in beignets and Civil War–era coffee.[279]

1872

A skiff pulled ashore and the queen stepped out. A cry went up—*Marie Laveau!* Three hundred black, white and mixed-race celebrants gathered at Lake Pontchartrain for the annual voodoo communion. The celebrants held hands and sang an arcane hymn: "Salma ma coupe ca."

The queen commanded each member of the crowd to find a piece of wood and pile the pieces into a pyre. *Make a wish when you throw on your piece.* A cauldron was set on the burning pyre, and Laveau began concocting her stew. The ingredients were a black snake cut into three; a cat, with its throat

Marie Laveau from *Century Magazine*, April 1886. *From Internet Archive.*

slashed; and a rooster, alive, with its head bound to its feet. Laveau and her assistants spoke over the brew: "Mam'selle Marie chauffez ca."

At midnight, the three hundred celebrants waded into the lake for a voodoo baptism. They climbed out, sang, and danced for an hour. Then a conch shell blew, and everyone gathered for dinner. As the celebrants ate jambalaya, four naked black women danced around Laveau's cauldron. Another song was sung. In the early hours of the morning, hands lifted the cauldron and poured its liquor into a barrel. Laveau watched as the vessel was filled. "Pour lannee prochaine," she said, "for the next year."[280]

1906

Salvatore Lupo sat in his grocery. He was a typical Sicilian grocer, trying to make a living in a city that had seen a tremendous influx of Sicilians in the last decade. In the next decade, a number of his fellow grocers would be dead, victims of a deranged axeman. But now, Salvatore had other reasons to worry. Bleary-eyed and with less sleep than usual, he anxiously awaited the lunch hour.

Day after day, Lupo had watched his fellow Sicilian dockworkers and truck farmers sit on crates during their lunch break with trays of bread, cheese, ham, salami and olive salad. Others simply stood, holding the tray in one hand, eating with the other. The industrious and creative Lupo had an idea. He took all the ingredients, mixed them together and put them between two pieces of sesame-seeded Sicilian bread. His creation would come to be known as the muffaletta.

More than one hundred years later, the muffuletta is New Orleans's most famous sandwich. It features salami, capicola, ham, provolone, emmentaler cheese and olive salad, all between thick, soft pieces of bread.[281]

1925

The twenty-seven-year-old unknown but talented poet searching to find his voice sat in his apartment at 624 Pirate's Alley. He had put in a good day's work, but now he was bored. He watched as passersby strolled along the alley outside, most pausing to look at the grandeur of St. Louis Cathedral.

Then the writer had an idea. He walked across his room and retrieved his BB gun. He sighted it at the most offensive looking gawker and took a pot shot at him. The writer got off a couple more shots, then ducked beneath his window.

He walked to the improvised bar and began to make himself a drink, content to let the other potential victims wander in peace. Normally, he would prefer a mint julep, his drink of choice. But this was New Orleans. He poured some rye whiskey into a glass and added a dash of absinthe and Peychaud's Bitters. When he stirred in a bit of sugar, he took the Sazerac and sat at his desk.

William Faulkner then refilled his pipe and got back to work.[282]

1929

Bennie and Clovis Martin had put in their time driving streetcars in New Orleans. They had quit the business to open a restaurant, but they still had a soft spot in their hearts for streetcar workers. So, when the carmen's union went on strike in 1929, the Martin brothers wrote to the striking union men, saying, "We are with you heart and soul. At any time you are around the French Market, don't forget to drop in at Martin's Coffee Stand and Restaurant...our meal is free to any members of Division 194."

Po-Boy Limbo at the 2007 Po-Boy Festival. *From Infrogmation of New Orleans.*

When the carmen had gone on strike, their incomes had ceased, and hunger was a real worry. The Martin brothers partnered with a Sicilian immigrant named John Gendusa to come up with the perfect meal to feed the striking workers. Cheap and filling, the key to the meal lay in a three-foot-long, uniformly thick bread loaf that Gendusa called "the special." Gendusa took the idea for the loaf from bread he had seen Sicilian bakers making when he was a child.

The men made sandwiches from loaves and handed them out to the "poor boys" on strike. The sandwich became popular, and soon other restaurants in the city were selling their versions. Gendusa and the Martin brothers had invented the po' boy.[283]

1943

Denton W. Crocker, a young army biologist who would soon be fighting malaria in New Guinea, sat alone at a table at Tujague's, wondering where the restaurant's menu was. There was none, he learned. He'd be eating the same thing as everyone else. Fine by him, he thought. The Massachusetts native had grown to love New Orleans cuisine, and he wanted to try one of the city's oldest restaurants before he had to ship out for the Pacific.

Crocker asked for a glass of port, deciding restraint was not in order. Tujague's had never been a place for restraint. Since opening in the 1850s, the French proprietors had served meals in several courses.

His first plate arrived—shrimp remoulade. The shrimp were cold, sharp, spicy. The intense flavors came from Creole mustard, lemon juice and cayenne pepper. Next came broiled crab with lemon and tomato. Then, the restaurant's famous beef brisket, boiled with aromatics and served with horseradish. Crocker sipped his port, taking mental notes of the meal. He had to tell Jean-Marie about this.

A strange old man took the seat opposite him. His name was the Judge, he said. He'd been eating at Tujague's every night for six years. Crocker and the Judge chatted—a young Yankee soldier and an old New Orleans eccentric.

Crocker's waiter delivered a plate of mocha cake and a cup of coffee to his table. He looked around the dining room and noticed that in New Orleans, people drank their coffee with spoons. Strange.

Crocker finished his dessert and looked at the Judge. Yes, he could see why a man would want to eat here every night.[284]

1940s–1950s

He sat at the bar. The room was spinning, but he ordered another drink anyway, a Vieux Carre, featuring Benedictine, bitters—Peychaud's and Agnostura—rye whiskey, vermouth and cognac.

It was only his second drink, but the room was spinning, just as the owner intended, one revolution of the bar every fifteen minutes. Hence its name, the Carousel Bar.

The little man next to him was experiencing the same spinning. But that might have been because the Vieux Carre in front of him was not his second drink. Normally, he drank screwdrivers, but tonight he imbibed the bar's native intoxicant, quite a few of them. He was babbling on about having been born just upstairs in one of the decadent rooms of the Hotel Monteleone. His voice became shriller and more agitated as he tried to convince his friend of the veracity of his claims.

But the older, dapper man was no longer listening. He was focused on finding the right words for one of the plays he was working on. He was also staring at the seductive young man spinning opposite him across the bar.

Tennessee Williams ordered a third Vieux Carre and another for his friend Truman Capote.[285]

1995

Tim was enjoying himself upstairs at Lafitte in Exile. He felt good. Really good. Cocaine tended to have that effect.

He tried to do it only on the weekends, but that was tough. He began to rely on the coping mechanism. Several years ago, his parents had intercepted some gay magazines that a friend had sent him through the mail. His mother exploded. She gave him the silent treatment for a week, then demanded that he seek psychiatric help. Instead, Tim moved to New Orleans. He used cocaine to cope with his pain. He used Lafitte's in Exile for acceptance, companionship and potentially love.

Normally, Tim just hung out and enjoyed mingling upstairs, but then there was the night with Rodeo Bob. Tim and Bob hit it off instantly. While others were cruising the notorious pool table, the newest couple slipped into the ladies' room. Afterward, Tim brought his fling back to his place.

Tim would be back at Lafitte's the next weekend and the next. His fellow shunned and ostracized would be there waiting for him. And then there would always be the cocaine.[286]

2005

The *New York Times* columnist stared into the flaming bowl of brandy-infused coffee and saw clarity. This, he would tell Americans a week later, is the "exuberance of the feast."

The columnist, Toronto-born David Brooks, had traveled to New Orleans and was dining at Antoine's with a group of friends. The party ate a "remorseless avalanche of delicious food" that included practically every delicacy you can find at a restaurant: oysters, foie gras, lobster, steak and crab. For dessert, they ate a basketball-sized meringue pie and drank cups of "devil's brew," the flaming, brandy/coffee mix that had triggered Brooks's epiphany.

Brooks calculated the total calories of the meal at a perhaps exaggerated (or perhaps not) eighteen thousand. After consuming his bacchanalian meal, Brooks realized that American life was too focused on restraint, well-being and productivity. "Smoking is now a worse evil than six of the Ten Commandments," he wrote.

Life had grown dull. "But," he concluded, "at least we have New Orleans. No matter how dull and responsible you become, an alternative and much stranger moral universe is always just one slippery step away."

2019

Hour by hour, the river rose inch by inch.

It was May 2019, and the U.S. Army Corps of Engineers was preparing to do something it had never done before. The corps would open the Bonnet Carré Spillway for the *second* time that year. The spillway was a last-ditch effort to spare New Orleans from flooding. Opening it would divert a part of the river away from the city and into Lake Pontchartrain. The volume of the river would be significantly reduced by the time it reached New Orleans and its levees.[287]

The rain had poured, and the river had risen six inches in the previous twenty-four hours. The corps took action. Workers set about removing, one by one, the thousands of creosoted wooden "needles" that acted as a barrier between the Mississippi and the plain connecting Lake Pontchartrain. As each needle was hoisted by cranes, more water poured through the spillway in foamy jets.[288]

The diversion worked. New Orleans was safe. But as water poured into Lake Pontchartrain and then into the Mississippi Sound, it became apparent that there was another problem. The sound, which was traditionally a saltwater body, had been filled almost completely with freshwater. The oysters, crabs, shrimp and fish that had fed New Orleans for centuries were being killed or pushed out.

By the time the corps of engineers closed Bonnet Carré Spillway in July, the damage had been done. The spillway had been diverting Mississippi River water into Lake Pontchartrain and Mississippi Sound for months. New Orleans was spared flooding, but it came with a cost. Shrimpers in the sound reported their worst harvest in decades. The shrimp catch was down 60 percent. The crab catch was down 40 percent. But hardest hit were the oysters. They had been all but wiped out.[289]

Later in 2019

The old friends sat at a high table near the bar as the music blared overhead. Coop's Place was always loud and always packed and always worth every penny. The two had been walking around the Quarter after a visit to "Sweetie" at the National Shrine of Our Lady of Prompt Succor on State Street. Now they were hungry.

Soon after arriving at Coop's, a smorgasbord of New Orleans staples was placed before them: seafood gumbo made from a dark roux, French market vegetables, crab claws, shrimp, oysters and, of course, okra; rabbit and sausage jambalaya; marinated lamb ribs served with a red pepper jelly dipping sauce; Cajun fried chicken; red beans and rice; and two Abita Wrought Iron IPAs.

They ate and discussed the allure of the Crescent City and how it was so easy to be drawn into its orbit. An hour later, the two sophisticated, smart, attractive and rich gentlemen paid their tab, walked down Decatur and said goodbye to the tragic, beautiful, always exotic New Orleans.

The French Market, circa 1906. *From Library of Congress.*

Josh Foreman punched GPS coordinates into his phone, and Ryan Starrett shifted into drive. The two writer friends set out for their next destination: Dallas, Texas.[290]

NOTES

Chapter 1

1. Barbeau, "Folk-Songs of French Canada," 172–73. Verses from "La Plainte du Coureur-des-bois" ("The Complaint of the Runner of the Woods") appear throughout the chapter. The song was a Canadian-made folk song written by the first French people to explore North America, likely being sung in the forests and along the rivers of North America when Andre Penicaut arrived on the Gulf Coast.
2. Penicaut, *Fleur de Lys*, 1–20.
3. Ibid., 16–17.
4. Bosher, "Imperial Environment," 57–60.
5. There has been some confusion whether Penicaut joined the first Iberville expedition to Louisiana in 1698, the second Iberville expedition in 1699 or both. Penicaut wrote in his memoir that he was with Iberville on his first journey in 1698.
6. Coker et al., "Spanish Pensacola.
7. Penicaut, *Fleur de Lys*; Hamilton, "Settlement," 137–38.
8. Penicaut, *Fleur de Lys*, 18.
9. Ibid., 25.
10. Ibid., 164–65.
11. Ibid., 34–40.
12. Ibid., 14.
13. Ibid., 48–49.

14. Ibid., 107–108.
15. Ibid., 168–172.
16. Kendall, *History of New Orleans*, 3–5.
17. "Some Southern Cities," *Records of the Catholic Historical Society of Philadelphia*, 201–203. Includes an excerpt from Darby's manuscript.
18. Gayarré, *History of Louisiana*, 49–50.
19. Penicaut, *Fleur de Lys*, 231–235.
20. Ibid., 235–36.
21. Ibid., 244–47.
22. Ibid., 183–91.
23. Ibid., 251–53.
24. Ibid., 253.
25. "Some Southern Cities," *Records of the Catholic Historical Society of Philadelphia*, 201–203.
26. "New Orleans: Early History," *Littell's Living Age*.
27. Campbell, "New Orleans in Early Days," 31.
28. "Some Southern Cities," *Records of the Catholic Historical Society of Philadelphia*, 201–203.
29. Penicaut, *Fleur de Lys*, 35–36.

Chapter 2

30. Clark, *Voices from an Early*, 63.
31. Ibid., 58.
32. Ibid., 56.
33. Ibid., 68.
34. Saxon, *Fabulous New Orleans*, 106.
35. Myers, *True Story of Pierre*, 173–74.
36. Saxon, *Fabulous New Orleans*, 110.
37. Caillot, *Company Man*, 123.
38. Myers, *True Story of Pierre*, 241–45, 281–85.
39. Dumont, *Memoir of Lieutenant Dumont*, 96; Caillot, *Company Man*, 148.
40. *Louisiana Historical Quarterly*. Reader, the trial of Michel Degout is a fascinating one. Degout obviously proclaimed his innocence. It was a simple case of self-defense, he claimed. It might have been. After reading the three court transcripts—Natchitoches (January 2, 1766) and New Orleans (January 29 and February 1, 1766)—I have written the story as if Marie Dardanne's version (and several other witnesses) of the events

represented reality. Degout's version, of course, was radically different. Again, he might have been telling the truth. I happen to side with the six judges who found him guilty. I urge you to come to your own conclusion.

41. King, *Jean Baptiste*, 138.

42. Penicaut, *Fleur de Lys*, 240.

43. Myers, *True Story of Pierre*, 33.

44. Ibid., 31–32.

45. Sublette, *World That Made*, 32–33.

Chapter 3

46. This is an imaginative retelling of an event that occurred many times between Pierre Lafitte Marie Villard.

47. Marie Villard exemplified an eighteenth century placee. Because of her black bloodlines, she could not enter into a standard marriage with a white man. Hence, the plaçage relationship between her and Pierre Lafitte.

48. Groom, *Patriotic Fire*, 102–3.

49. Ibid., 103–4.

50. W. Davis, *Pirates Laffite*, 188–93.

51. Ibid., 209.

52. Ibid., 208–209.

53. Kilmeade and Yaeger, *Andrew Jackson*, 125, 210, 227. The Ursuline nuns, true to their word, did treat many of the wounded after the battle—even a few British soldiers. Andrew Jackson, after his stunning victory, and after hearing of the services rendered and the vigil of the nuns, visited their convent to express his personal gratitude.

54. Ashe, *Travels in America*, 345–46.

55. Martineau, *Society in America*, 326–27.

56. Charters, *Trumpet around the Corner*, 31.

57. Latour, *Historical Memoir*, 186. Letter from Edward Nicholls to Mr. Laffite, or the commandant of Barataria, August 31, 1814.

58. W. Davis, *Pirates Laffite*, 174.

59. Latour, *Historical Memoir*, 189. Letter from Jean Laffite to Mr. Blanque, September 4, 1814.

60. W. Davis, *Pirates Laffite*, 525–26.

61. Ibid., 64.

62. Ibid., 74.

63. Ibid., 87.

64. Ibid., 157–58.

65. Ibid., 158–59.

66. Ibid., 161.

67. Ibid., 175.

68. Ibid., 176. Letter from Diego Morphy, Spanish consul, to Juan Ruiz de Apodaca, captain general in Cuba, September 5, 1814.

69. Latour, *Historical Memoir*, 58.

70. W. Davis, *Pirates Laffite*, 216.

71. Latour, *Historical Memoir*, 59.

72. Parton, *Life of Andrew Jackson*, 237–38.

Chapter 4

73. Solomon, *Civil War Diary*, 314.

74. Ibid., 311.

75. Ibid., 80.

76. Ibid., 106–7.

77. Ibid., 110, 112.

78. Butler, *Butler's Book*, 223.

79. Hearn, *When the Devil*, 87.

80. Solomon, *Civil War Diary*, 370.

81. Ibid., 407.

82. Ibid., 424–25.

83. Ibid., 419–20.

84. Hearn, *When the Devil*, 101.

85. Ibid., 102.

86. Solomon, *Civil War Diary*, 369–70.

87. Butler, *Private and Official Correspondence*, 483.

88. Hearn, *When the Devil*, 136.

89. Solomon, *Civil War Diary*, 301.

90. Ibid., 273.

91. Ibid., 264.

92. Butler, *Butler's Book*, 244.

93. Ibid., 244.

94. Solomon, *Civil War Diary*, 401.

95. Ibid., 408, 279.

96. He assumed she was pregnant.

97. Hearn, *When the Devil*, 169–170; Phillips, "Journal of Mrs. Eugenia." These sources provide the story of Eugenia Phillips's incarceration at Ship Island.

98. Solomon, *Civil War Diary*, 429-430.

99. Hearn, *When the Devil*, 219–20.

100. Ibid., 221.

101. Ibid., 196.

102. Andrew Jackson's continuance of martial law after the Battle of New Orleans rubbed many citizens the wrong way.

103. Solomon, *Civil War Diary*, 440–43.

Chapter 5

104. "Shot to Death," *Daily Picayune*; "Fifth Day of the Trial," *Daily Picayune*; "Sixth Day of the Trial," *Daily Picayune*. The story of Andrew H. "Cap" Murphy's murder in broad daylight first appeared the day after in the *Daily Picayune*.

105. "Gaiety Theatre," *New Orleans Republican*; "Judicial Advertisement," *Daily Picayune*. The contents of the theater were sold at public auction by judicial order in 1879.

106. "Murphy-Cooney Encounter," *Daily Picayune*; "Crooked Cooney," *New Orleans Daily Democrat*.

107. "Election Case," *Daily Picayune*; "Second Recorder's Court," *Daily Picayune*.

108. "Ford and Murphy," *Times-Democrat*.

109. "Shot to Death," *Daily Picayune*.

110. "Number Twenty," *Daily Picayune*.

111. "Base Ball," *New Orleans Democrat*.

112. "Pugilism," *Daily Picayune*.

113. "First Ward to the Front," *New Orleans Democrat*; Asbury, *French Quarter*, 395.

114. Asbury, *French Quarter*, 356–57, 395–96.

115. "Ford and Murphy," *Times-Democrat*.

116. Ibid.

117. Ibid.

118. Ibid.

119. Skinner, "How Do You Define."

120. "Shot to Death," *Daily Picayune*; "Fourth Day's Proceedings," *Daily Picayune*; "Fifth Day of the Trial," *Daily Picayune*.

121. "Men of Nerve," *Times-Democrat*; "Fireman's Festival," *Times-Democrat*; "Fourth Ward," *New Orleans Republican*; 1880 U.S. census; 1900 U.S. census; "Ford and Murphy," *Daily Picayune*.

122. "Judge and Special," *Times-Democrat*.

123. "Second Recorder's Court," *Daily Picayune*.

124. "Murdered Murphy," *Daily Picayune*.

125. "Carnival of Blood," *Daily Picayune*.

126. "To-Day's Criminal Trial," *Daily Picayune*.

127. Ibid.

128. "We predict…," *Alexandria Democrat*.

129. "Murdered Murphy," *Daily Picayune*.

130. "Thomas J. Ford," *Daily Picayune*.

131. "Mistrial," *Daily Picayune*.

132. "Murdered Murphy," *Daily Picayune*.

133. Ibid.

134. "Ford's Day," *Daily Picayune*.

135. "Thomas J. Ford," *Daily Picayune*.

136. Ibid.

Chapter 6

137. M. Davis, *Axeman of New Orleans*, 51.

138. Wells-Barnett, *Mob Rule*, 669–74.

139. Krist, *Empire of Sin*, 88–90.

140. Reef, *This Our Dark Country*, 11–14.

141. Ibid., 15–25.

142. "Late Expedition from New-Orleans," 153–54.

143. Ibid.; Dennis, "Mississippi Colonial Experience."

144. "Late Expedition from New-Orleans," 153–54.

145. Huberich, *Political and Legislative History*.

146. Krist, *Empire of Sin*, 90–91.

147. Ibid., 91–94.

148. Huffman, *Mississippi in Africa*, 155–65.

149. Ibid.

150. Ibid.

151. Wells-Barnett, *Mob Rule*, 45–51.

152. Ibid., 128

153. Ibid., 203.

154. Ibid., 248.

155. Ibid.,465–76.

156. Krist, *Empire of Sin*, 99–104.

157. Ibid., 105.

158. Ibid., 105.

159. Wells-Barnett, *Mob Rule*, 753–59.

160. Ibid., 767.

Chapter 7

161. Krist, *Empire of Sin*, 77, 125–26, 137.

162. M. Davis, *Axeman of New Orleans*, 14–15.

163. Krist, *Empire of Sin*, 258.

164. Ibid., 107–20.

165. Krist, *Empire of Sin*, 196; Charters, *Trumpet around the Corner*, 86.

166. M. Davis, *Axeman of New Orleans*, 21–24.

167. Ibid., 56–59.

168. Armstrong, *Satchmo*, 86–88.

169. Karst, "Who Killed New Orleans' Police Chief."

170. M. Davis, *Axeman of New Orleans*, 86–90.]

171. Anderson, *Guadalcanal*, 288; Krist, *Empire of Sin*, 282.

172. *New Orleans Times-Picayune*, June 20, 1918.

173. M. Davis, *Axeman of New Orleans*, 123–26.

174. Ibid., 5.

175. Ibid., 10.

176. Ibid., 157–58.

177. Armstrong, *Satchmo*, 150–55.

178. M. Davis, *Axeman of New Orleans*, 217–19

Chapter 8

179. "New Orleans Debacle," *Labor Age*, 5; "Hundreds Riot in Streets," *Times-Picayune*; "Dynamite Blast Hurts Passenger," *Times-Picayune*.

180. Allan, "Call of Duty," 21–24, 45.

181. Hennick and Charlton, *Streetcars of New Orleans*, 6–7; Mulla, "Harness Electricity."

182. Hennick and Charlton, *Streetcars of New Orleans*, 7–32.

183. Wilcox, *American City*, 28–29.

184. Norwood, *Strikebreaking and Intimidation*, 34–35.

185. Ibid.; Leigh, "New Orleans Debacle," 3–6.

186. Norwood, *Strikebreaking and Intimidation*, 34–35.

187. Leigh, "New Orleans Debacle," 3–6.

188. Ibid., 37.

189. "Striking Carman Shot," *Times-Picayune*.

190. Ibid.

191. Ibid; Leigh, "New Orleans Debacle," 5.

192. "Dynamite Plot Seen," *Times-Picayune*.

193. "Hundreds Riot in Streets," *Times-Picayune*.

194. "All-Day Riot," *New York Times*.

195. "Hundreds Riot in Streets," *Times-Picayune*.

196. Ibid.

197. "Strikers Bomb Barns," *Crowley Daily Signal*.

198. "Dynamite Hidden in Headquarters," *Times-Picayune*.

199. "Strikers Bomb Barns," *Crowley Daily Signal*.

200. "Stolen Dynamite May Have Figured," *Times-Picayune*.

201. "Boatner to Pass on Jitney," *Times-Picayune*.

202. "Bombs Roar as N.O. Car," *Crowley Daily Signal*.

203. "Dynamite Thrown into Street Car," *Alexandria Daily Town Talk*.

204. "Jitney Operators Await Decision," *Alexandria Weekly Town Talk*.

205. "New Orleans Car Bombings," *Shreveport Times*.

206. "Decision of Judge in Jitney," *Alexandria Daily Town Talk*.

207. "Carmen Vote to End Strike," *Alexandria Daily Town Talk*.

208. "New Orleans Car Bombings," *Shreveport Times*.

209. "New Jitneymobile Law," *Herald*; "Jitney Bus Regulation," *Harvard Law Review*, 437–38.

210. "New Jitneymobile Law," *Herald*; Leigh, "New Orleans Debacle," 3–6.

211. "N.O. City Hall Stormed," *Alexandria Daily Town Talk*.

212. "Almost 100 Arrested," *Alexandria Daily Town Talk*.

213. Leigh, "New Orleans Debacle," 3–6.

214. Ibid.

215. Hennick and Charlton, *Streetcars of New Orleans*, 39.

216. Allan, "Call of Duty," 6.

Chapter 9

217. Downs, "Terror in the Gulf."

218. "#Veteranoftheday," *Vantage Point*; Crocker, *My War on Mosquitoes*, 1–2.

219. Crocker, *My War on Mosquitoes*, 1–2.

220. Ibid., 3–8.

221. McCoy, "War Department Provisions," 12–13.

222. Crocker, *My War on Mosquitoes*, 15, 37.

223. Ibid., 34–37.

224. Centers for Disease Control, "Malaria."

225. Condon-Rall, "Army's War gainst Malaria," 129–30.

226. Anderson, *Guadalcanal*.

227. Crocker, "Malaria Survey."

228. McCoy, "War Department Provisions," 23–24.

229. Morison, *History of United States Naval*, 130.

230. Downs, "Terror in the Gulf."

231. Morison, *History of United States Naval*, 125–30.

232. Ibid.

233. Ibid., 135–37.

234. Cox, "Gulf of Mexico."

235. Blair, *Hitler's U-Boat War*, 578–79.

236. Ibid., 42, 60, 578–79.

237. Morison, *History of United States Naval*, 128.

238. Blair, *Hitler's U-Boat War*, 579–80.

239. Cox, "Gulf of Mexico," 66–69.

240. Crocker, *My War on Mosquitoes*, 46.

241. Ibid., 48.

242. Ibid., 47–48.

243. Ibid., 49–50.

244. Ibid., 49.

245. Ibid., 51.

246. Ibid., 55.

247. Crocker, "Malaria Survey."

248. Crocker, *My War on Mosquitoes*, 78–81.

249. Ibid., 85–86.

250. Crocker, *My War on Mosquitoes*, 85–86.

251. Wilkinson, "Cat Tales."

252. Morison, *History of United States Naval*, 202–65.

253. Ibid., 400–404.

254. Denton W. Crocker Collection; Masterson, *Malaria Project*.

Chapter 10

255. Williams, *Memoirs*, 2.
256. Williams, *Vieux Carre*. This story is an introduction and a summary of the play. The quotations are verbatim from Williams's original.
257. Ibid. From Robert Bray's introduction to *Vieux Carre*.
258. Ibid.
259. Williams, *Memoirs*, 75.
260. Delery, *Out for Queer Blood*, 101, 173; "Three Students Freed," *Daily Herald*.
261. Williams, *Memoirs*, 161.
262. Ibid., 241.
263. Ibid., 139.
264. Delery, *Out for Queer Blood*, 14; Perez and Palmquist, *In Exile*, 93–96; Fieseler, *Tinderbox*, 73–88.
265. Williams, *Memoirs*, 100.
266. Sears, *Rebels, Rubyfruit and Rhinestones*, 96–98; Perez and Palmquist, *In Exile*, 117–18.
267. Perez and Palmquist, *In Exile*, 31, 118. Perez and Palmquist substantiate their theory by citing the following studies: Amy Gluckman and Betsy Reed, *Homo Economics: Capitalism, Community, and Lesbian and Gay Life* (New York: Routledge, 1997); M.V. Lee Badgett, *Money, Myth, and Change The Economic Lives of Lesbians and Gay Men* (Chicago: University of Chicago Press, 2003); Robert Witeck and Wesley Combs, *Business Inside Out Capturing Millions of Brand Loyal Gay Customers* (Chicago: Kaplan Business, 2006); Alexandra Chasin, *Selling Out: The Gay and Lesbian Movement Goes to Market* (Basingstoke, England: Palgrave, 2001); and "Where Successful Advertising Meets LGBT Equality," AdRespect Advertising Education Program, www.commercialcloset.com.
268. Williams, *Memoirs*, 248.
269. "30 Years Ago Monday," CBS New York.
270. Perez and Palmquist, *In Exile*, 125–26.
271. Ibid., 129.

Chapter 11

272. Penicaut, *Fleur de Lys*, 24–25.

273. "Scraps from an Invalid's," *Flag of the Union*; "Some Southern Cities," *Records of the Catholic Historical Society of Philadelphia*, 201–3. The only historical source that mentions Madam Bangs is a traveler's log from 1835, which was published after the woman had died. According to the article, Madam Bangs looked over the log buildings of New Orleans in 1717, but most sources agree that construction on the city did not begin until 1718.

274. Charters, *Trumpet around the Corner*, 274–75; Sublette, *World That Made*, 8–11; Clark, *Voices from an Early*, 63.

275. Sublette, *World That Made*, 58, 61, 117, 118. This is an imaginative retelling of what a typical evening must have been like for the ex-slave turned executioner.

276. Fearon, *Sketches of America*, 270–78.

277. "Ordinance Concerning the Poydras," *True American*; Laskow, "For 15 Years."

278. "For Sale," *Daily Picayune*. Imagined scene based on a detailed advertisement for R.F. Nichols's store that appeared in an 1841 issue of the *Daily Picayune*.

279. Smith, "History of the Chicory Coffee," 233, 245, 248–49, 256.

280. "Voudouism," *Lancaster Intelligencer*.

281. M. Davis, *Axeman of New Orleans*, 35–36.

282. "William Faulkner's New Orleans," *Times-Picayune*. This is an imaginative retelling of an event that happened occasionally at what is today known as the Faulkner House. And yes, Faulkner did amuse himself by firing his BB gun at passersby.

283. Mizell-Nelson, "Po-Boy Sandwich."

284. Crocker, *My War on Mosquitoes*, 52–53; Tujague's Restaurant, "History"; Maloney, "Tujague's Boiled Shrimp."

285. Joe Gambino's Bakery, "The Drink That Spins." This scene is entirely fictional, but Tennessee Williams and Truman Capote were, in fact, good friends and both thoroughly enjoyed the Carousel Bar. (They both enjoyed their alcohol just as thoroughly.)

286. Perez and Palmquist, *In Exile*, 160–61.

287. "Mississippi River Flooding," *Newsweek*.

288. Mitchell, "Corps: Bonne Carre."

289. Blank, "Gulf Fisheries Suffer."

290. This day and lunch are historical. Most of the adjectives describing Foreman and Starrett are wishful thinking—especially the rich part. Although, if you enjoyed their book, tell your friends, or better yet, buy the book for them as a gift and help make the "rich" part a fact.

BIBLIOGRAPHY

Articles

Alexandria Daily Town Talk. "Almost 100 Arrested Under Jitney Law." August 17, 1929.

———. "Carmen Vote to End Strike, Add Provision." October 11, 1929.

———. "Decision of Judge in Jitney Case Is Awaited by Police." August 23, 1929.

———. "Dynamite Thrown into Street Car." September 13, 1929.

———. "N.O. City Hall Stormed by Mob." August 13, 1929.

Alexandria Democrat. "We predict...." February 4, 1885.

Alexandria Weekly Town Talk. "Jitney Operators Await Decision in New Orleans Case." November 9, 1929.

Blank, Christine. "Gulf Fisheries Suffer Major Losses; Recovery Underway." *Seafood Source,* September 6, 2019. https://www.seafoodsource.com.

CBS New York. "30 Years Ago Monday: Tennessee Williams Dies in Manhattan Hotel Suite." February 25, 2013. https://newyork.cbslocal.com.

Crowley Daily Signal. "Bombs Roar as N.O. Car Peace Fails." September 12, 1929.

———. "Strikers Bomb Barns, Burn 5 Cars in Riots." July 6, 1929.

Daily Herald. "Three Students Freed in Guide's Death." January 24, 1959.

Daily Picayune. "Carnival of Blood." December 3, 1884.

———. "An Election Case." November 8, 1879.

———. "The Ford Party on Trial—The Fifth Day of the Trial." February 25, 1885.

———. "The Ford Party on Trial—The Sixth Day of the Trial." February 26, 1885.

———. "Ford's Day at Baton Rouge." March 12, 1895.

———. "The Ford Trial—The Fourth Day's Proceedings." February 24, 1885.

———. "For Sale by the Subscribers." February 2, 1841.

———. "Judicial Advertisement." July 19, 1879.

———. "A Mistrial." February 10, 1885.

———. "Murdered Murphy." December 3, 1884.

———. "The Murphy-Cooney Encounter." January 17, 1879.

———. "Number Twenty." April 13, 1881.

———. "Pugilism." June 7, 1884.

———. "Second Recorder's Court." April 8, 1883.

———. "Shot to Death." December 2, 1884.

———. "Thomas J. Ford Will Soon Be Pardoned." March 10, 1895.

———. "To-Day's Criminal Trial." January 27, 1885.

Downs, Ray, Jr. "Terror in the Gulf." Interview by David Kindy. *World War II Magazine*. October 2018.

Flag of the Union. "Scraps from an Invalid's Log." June 18, 1835.

Herald. "The New Jitneymobile Law." April 29, 1915.

Karst, James. "Who Killed New Orleans' Police Chief 100 Years Ago?" *Times-Picayune*. August 7, 1917. Reprinted July 16, 2017. https://www.nola.com.

Lancaster Intelligencer. "Voudouism." July 17, 1872.

Laskow, Sarah. "For 15 Years, New Orleans Was Divided into Three Separate Cities." *Atlas Obscura*. January 6, 2017. https://www.atlasobscura.com.

Littell's Living Age. "New Orleans: Early History." April 4, 1846.

Maloney, Ann. "Tujague's Boiled Shrimp with White and Red Remoulade Recipe." *Times-Picayune*, April 30, 2016.

Mitchell, David J. "Corps: Bonne Carre Spillway Could open as Soon as Wednesday Due to Rising Mississippi, Rain." *Acadiana Advocate*, Februay 21, 2019.

New Orleans Daily Democrat. "Crooked Cooney." January 21, 1879.

New Orleans Democrat. "Base Ball." August 22, 1879.

———. "First Ward to the Front." July 11, 1880.

New Orleans Republican. "Fourth Ward." November 7, 1876.

———. "The Gaiety Theatre." November 6, 1875.

New Orleans Times-Picayune. June 20, 1918.

Newsweek. "Mississippi River Flooding: With New Orleans Levee Pressure Increasing, Bonne Carré Spillway Opened." May 11, 2019. https://www.newsweek.com.

New York Times. "All-Day Riot Marks New Orleans Strike; 2 Die, Hundreds Hurt." July 6, 1929.

Perez, Frank. "Killer Tricks." *Ambush Magazine*, September 24–October 7, 2013. http://www.ambushmag.com.

Shreveport Times. "New Orleans Car Bombings Now Total 64." January 3, 1930.

Smith, Annabelle. "The History of the Chicory Coffee Mix That New Orleans Made Its Own." *Smithsonian*, March 5, 2014. https://www.smithsonianmag.com.

Thevenot, Brian. "Boyfriend Cut Up Corpse, Cooked It." *Times-Picayune*, October 19, 2006.

Times-Democrat. "A Fireman's Festival." May 21, 1883.

———. "Ford and Murphy." March 13, 1886.

———. "Judge and Special." April 29, 1883.

———. "Men of Nerve." March 5, 1883.

Times-Picayune. "Boatner to Pass on Jitney Writ Petition Today." August 23, 1929.

———. "Dynamite Blast Hurts Passenger on Trolley Car." August 22, 1929.

———. "Dynamite Hidden in Headquarters, Striker Asserts." August 17, 1929.

———. "Dynamite Plot Seen in Switch Box Tampering." July 5, 1929.

———. "Hundreds Riot in Streets as Trolleys Attempt to Run." July 6, 1929.

———. "Stolen Dynamite May Have Figured in Car Explosion." August 23, 1929.

———. "Striking Carman Shot, Scores Hurt in Car Barn Riots." July 5, 1929.

———. "William Faulkner's New Orleans survives in French Quarter." https://www.nola.com.

True American. "An Ordinance Concerning the Poydras Street Market." September 27, 1838.

Wilkinson, Stephan, "Cat Tales: The Story of World War II's PBY Flying Boat." *Aviation History Magazine*, May 1, 2013.

Books

Anderson, Charles R. *Guadalcanal: The U.S. Army Campaigns of World War II*. Washington, D.C.: Army Center of Military History, 2004.

Armstrong, Louis. *Satchmo: My Life in New Orleans*. New York: Da Capo Press, 1986.

Asbury, Herbert. *The French Quarter: An Informal History of the New Orleans Underworld*. New York: Knopf, 1936.

Ashe, Thomas. *Travels in America, Performed in 1806, for the Purpose of Exploring the Rivers Alleghany, Monongahela, Ohio, and Mississippi, and Ascertaining the Produce and Condition of Their Banks and Vicinity*. New York: n.p., 1811.

Blair, Clay. *Hitler's U-Boat War*. New York: Random House, 1996.

Butler, Benjamin. *Butler's Book: Autobiography and Personal Reminiscences of Major-General Benjamin Butler*. Self-published, CreateSpace, 2014.

—————. *Private and Official Correspondence of Gen. Benjamin F. Butler During the Period of the Civil War: In Five Volumes*. Vol. 1, *April 1860–June 1862*. Norwood, MA: Plimpton Press, 1917.

Caillot, Marc-Antoine. *A Company Man: The Remarkable French-Atlantic Voyage of a Clerk for the Company of the Indies*. Edited by Erin M. Greenwald. New Orleans, LA: Historic New Orleans Collection, 2013.

Charters, Samuel. *A Trumpet around the Corner: The Story of New Orleans Jazz*. Jackson: University Press of Mississippi, 2008.

Clark, Emily. *Voices from an Early American Convent: Marie Hachard and the New Orleans Ursulines, 1727–1760*. Baton Rouge: Louisiana State University Press, 2009.

Coker, William S., et al. "Spanish Pensacola 1698–1763." In *Florida: From the Beginning to 1992*, 201–203. Houston, TX: Pioneer Publications, 1991.

Crocker, Denton W. *My War on Mosquitoes, 1942–1945*. Saratoga Springs, NY: Skidmore College, 1997.

Davis, Miriam C. *The Axeman of New Orleans: The True Story*. Chicago: Chicago Review Press, 2017.

Davis, William C. *The Pirates Laffite: The Treacherous World of the Corsairs of the Gulf*. Orlando, FL: Harcourt, 2005.

Dawdy, Shannon Lee. *The Burden of Louis Congo and the Evolution of Savagery in Colonial Louisiana*. Durham, NC: Duke University Press, 2006.

Delery, Clayton. *Out for Queer Blood: The Murder of Fernando Rios and the Failure of New Orleans Justice*. Jefferson, NC: Exposit, 2017.

Dumont, Jean-Francois-Benjamin. *The Memoir of Lieutenant Dumont, 1715–1747: A Sojourner in the French Atlantic*. Chapel Hill: University of North Carolina Press, 2012.

Fearon, Henry Bradshaw. *Sketches of America*. London: Longman, 1818.

Fieseler, Robert W. *Tinderbox: The Untold Story of the Up Stairs Lounge Fire and the Rise of Gay Liberation*. New York: Liveright Publishing, 2018.

Gayarré, Charles. *History of Louisiana: The French Domination*. Vol. 1. New York: Redfield, 1854.

Groom, Winston. *Patriotic Fire: Andrew Jackson and Laffite at the Battle of New Orleans*. New York: Vintage, 2007.

Heaney, Sister Jane Francis, O.S.U. *A Century of Pioneering: A History of the Ursuline Nuns in New Orleans 1727–1837*. Chelsea, MI: Ursuline Sisters of New Orleans, Louisiana, 1993.

Hearn, Chester G. *When the Devil Came Down to Dixie: Ben Butler in New Orleans*. Baton Rouge: Louisiana State University Press, 1997.

Hennick, Louis C., and Charlton, Elbridge H. *The Streetcars of New Orleans*. New Orleans: Jackson Square Press, 2005.

Huberich, Charles Henry. *The Political and Legislative History of Liberia*. New York: Central Book, 1947.

Huffman, Alan. *Mississippi in Africa*. New York: Gotham Books, 2004.

Kendall, John Smith. *History of New Orleans*. Vol. 1. Chicago: Lewis Publishing, 1922.

Kilmeade, Brian, and Don Yaeger. *Andrew Jackson and the Miracle of New Orleans*. New York: Sentinel, 2017.

King, Grace. *Jean Baptiste Le Moyne Sieur De Bienville*. N.p.: Wentworth Press, 2019.

Krist, Gary. *Empire of Sin: A Story of Sex, Jazz, Murder, and the Battle for Modern New Orleans*. New York: Crown, 2014.

Latour, Arsene Lacarriere. *Historical Memoir of the War in West Florida and Louisiana in 1814–15*. Gainesville: University Press of Florida, 1999.

Martineau, Harriet. *Society in America*. Vol. 2. London: Saunders and Otley, 1837.

Masterson, Karen M. *The Malaria Project: The U.S. Government's Secret Mission to Find a Miracle Cure*. New York: Penguin, 2014.

McCoy, Oliver R., MD. "War Department Provisions for Malaria Control." Chapter 2 in *Preventive Medicine in World War II*. Vol. 6, *Communicable Diseases*. Edited by John Boyd Coates Jr. Washington, D.C.: Office of the Surgeon General, 1963.

Morison, Samuel Eliot. *History of United States Naval Operations in World War II*. Vol. 1, *The Battle of the Atlantic*. Annapolis, MD: Naval Institute Press, 1947.

Myers, Kenneth N. *1729: The True Story of Pierre and Marie Mayeux, the Natchez Massacre, and the Settlement of French Louisiana*. Denison, TX: Mayeux Press, 2017.

Nevils, Rene Pol, and Deborah George Hardy. *Ignatius Rising: The Life of John Kennedy Toole*. Baton Rouge: Louisiana State University Press, 2001.

Norwood, Stephen Harlan. *Strikebreaking and Intimidation: Mercenaries and Masculinity in Twentieth-Century America*. Chapel Hill: University of North Carolina Press, 2002.

Parton, James. *Life of Andrew Jackson*. 3 vols. New York: Mason Brothers, 1861.

Penicaut, Andre. *Fleur de Lys and Calumet: Being the Penicaut Narrative of French Adventure in Louisiana*. Translated and edited by Richebourg Gaillard McWilliams. Tuscaloosa: University of Alabama Press, 1953.

Perez, Frank, and Jeffrey Palmquist. *In Exile: The History and Lore Surrounding New Orleans Gay Culture and Its Oldest Gay Bar*. Hulford, Scotland: LL Publications, 2012.

Reef, Catherine. *This Our Dark Country: The American Settlers of Liberia*. New York: Clarion Books, 2002.

Saxon, Lyle. *Fabulous New Orleans*. Gretna, LA: Pelican Publishing, 1988.

Sears, James T. *Rebels, Rubyfruit, and Rhinestones: Queering Space in the Stonewall South*. Iscataway, NJ: Rutgers University Press, 2001.

Solomon, Clara. *The Civil War Diary of Clara Solomon: Growing Up in New Orleans 1861–1862*. Edited by Elliott Ashkenazi. Baton Rouge: Louisiana State University Press, 1995.

Sublette, Ned. *The World That Made New Orleans: From Spanish Silver to Congo Square*. Chicago: Lawrence Hill, 2009.

Toole, John Kennedy. *A Confederacy of Dunces*. New York: Grove Press, 1980.

Townend, Johnny. *Let the Faggots Burn: The Upstairs Lounge Fire*. Self-published, booklocker.com, 2011.

Wells-Barnett, Ida B. *Mob Rule in New Orleans: Robert Charles and His Fight to the Death, the Story of His Life, Burning Human Beings Alive, Other Lynching Statistics*. N.p., 1900.

Wilcox, Delos F. *The American City: A Problem in Democracy*. New York: Macmillan, 1904.

Williams, Tennessee. *Memoirs*. New York: Doubleday, 1975.

———. *Vieux Carre*. New York: New Directions, 2000.

Journals

Allan, Shaun. "Call of Duty—Modern Warfare: The Effects of Landmines and IEDs on British Troops in Afghanistan Post 2001." *Baltic Security and Defence Review* 13, no. 2 (2011): 21–45.

Anderson, Gene H. "The Genesis of King Oliver's Creole Jazz Band." *American Music* 12, no. 3 (Fall 1994): 283–303. https://scholarship.richmond.edu.

Barbeau, Marius. "Folk-Songs of French Canada." *Music & Letters* 13, no. 2 (1932): 172–173.

Bosher, J.F. "The Imperial Environment of French Trade with Canada, 1660–1685." *English Historical Review* 108, no. 426 (January 1993): 51–81.

Campbell, Edna F. "New Orleans in Early Days." *Geographical Review* 10, no. 1 (July 1920): 31–36.

Condon-Rall, Mary Ellen. "The Army's War Against Malaria: Collaboration in Drug Research During World War II." *Armed Forces and Society* 21, no. 1 (1994): 129–30.

Cox, William J., "The Gulf of Mexico: A Forgotten Frontier in the 1980s." *Naval War College Review* 40, no. 3 (1987): 66–69.

Crocker, Denton W. "Malaria Survey and Malaria Control Detachments in the South-West Pacific Area in World War II." *Papua New Guinea Medical Journal* 52, no. 1–2 (2009): 54–68.

Hamilton, Peter J. "The French Settlement of the Mississippi Valley." *American Historical Magazine and Tennessee Historical Society Quarterly* 7, no. 2 (April 1902): 136–147.

"Jitney Bus Regulation." *Harvard Law Review* 29, no. 4 (1916): 437–38.

"Late Expedition from New-Orleans." *African Repository and Colonial Journal* (May 1, 1835): 153–54.

Leigh, J.W. "The New Orleans Debacle." *Labor Age* 17, no. 12 (December 1929): 3–6.

Louisiana Historical Quarterly 3, no. 4 (October 1920).

Skinner, Stan. "How Do You Define Perfection?" *Texas Fish and Game* 33, no. 11 (2017): 56–58.

"Some Southern Cities (in the U.S.) About 1750." *Records of the Catholic Historical Society of Philadelphia* 10, no. 2 (1899): 201–207.

Websites

Centers for Disease Control and Prevention. "Malaria." Frequently Asked Questions. US Department of Health and Human Services. www.cdc.gov.

Joe Gambino's Bakery. "The Drink That Spins: The Vieux Carre Cocktail." The Carousel Cocktail: History of the Vieux Carre. November 6, 2019. https://gambinos.com.

Mizell-Nelson, Michael. "Po-Boy Sandwich." *New Orleans Historical.* https://neworleanshistorical.org.

Phillips, Eugenia Levy. "Journal of Mrs. Eugenia Levy Phillips, 1861–1862." Jewish-American History Foundation. Accessed April 12, 2019. http://www.jewish-history.com.

Tujague's Restaurant and Bar. "History." https://tujaguesrestaurant.com.

"#VeteranOfTheDay Denton W. Crocker Sr. and Denton 'Mogie' W. Crocker Jr." *Vantage Point* (blog). U.S. Department of Veterans Affairs. March 26, 2019. https://www.blogs.va.gov.

Other

1880 U.S. census. Orleans Parish. New Orleans, LA. June 8, 1880.

1900 U.S. census. Orleans Parish. New Orleans, LA. June 2, 1900.

Dennis, Dawn A. "The Mississippi Colonial Experience in Liberia, 1829–1861: The Racial Ideology of Uplift Suasion." Draft, 2018. https://www.academia.edu.

Denton W. Crocker Collection. Veterans History Project. American Folklife Center. Library of Congress.

Mulla Brittany, Anne. "Harness Electricity, Free the Mules: Animal Rights and the Electrification of the Streetcars in New Orleans." Master's thesis, University of New Orleans, 2010.